Higher
Modern
Studies

How to Pass

SECOND EDITION

HIGHER

Modern Studies

Frank Cooney, Kenneth Hannah,
Mary Clare McGinty and Steph O'Reilly

HODDER
GIBSON
AN HACHETTE UK COMPANY

The Publishers would like to thank the following for permission to reproduce copyright material:

Photo credits

p.6 top © Marco Saracco – Fotolia.com, bottom © roger Pilkington – Fotolia.com; **p.10** left © Duncan Bryceland/REX/Shutterstock, right © REX/Shutterstock; **p.20** © Andy Buchanan/AFP/Getty Images; **p.26** © Ken McKay/ITV/REX/Shutterstock; **p.39** © Robert Perry/REX/Shutterstock; **p.42** © Douglas Carr/ALAMY STOCK PHOTO; **p.43** © Jeff J Mitchell/Getty Images; **p.51** © Photographee.eu/Shutterstock.com; **p.54** © britstock images ltd/ALAMY STOCK PHOTO; **p.59** © Matt West/BPI/REX/Shutterstock; **p.61** © David Levenson/ALAMY STOCK PHOTO; **p.62** top © Scottish Children's Reporter Administration, bottom © Children's Hearings Scotland; **p.67** © Dominic Cocozza; **p.68** © LEON NEAL/AFP/Getty Images; **p.74** © User:Wapcaplet/Wikimedia Commons (http://creativecommons.org/licenses/by-sa/3.0/deed.en); **p.81** left © Edward Parker/ALAMY STOCK PHOTO, right © Denis Tangney Jr/Getty Images; **p.87** top Courtesy of PhiLiP via Wikimedia Commons, Translation by Peter17 (http://creativecommons.org/licenses/by-sa/3.0/deed.en), bottom © ZUMA/REX/Shutterstock; **p.97** © djama – Fotolia.com; **p.98** © David South/ALAMY STOCK PHOTO; **p.103** © STR/Stringer/Getty Images; **p.106** top © kosmozoo/DigitalVision Vectors/Getty Images, bottom left © African National Congress, bottom right © National Freedom Party; **p.107** top left © Democratic Alliance, top right © United Democratic Movement, centre left © Economic Freedom Fighters, centre right © Congress of the People, bottom centre left © Inkatha Freedom Party, bottom left © MIKE HUTCHINGS/AFP/Getty Images; **p.109** © Giordano Stolley/ALAMY STOCK PHOTO; **p.111** © Monkey Business Images/Shutterstock.com; **p.114** © sirtravelalot/Shutterstock.com; **p.129** © Oxfam.

Acknowledgements

Please see **p.160**.

Every effort has been made to trace all copyright holders, but if any have been inadvertently overlooked, the Publishers will be pleased to make the necessary arrangements at the first opportunity.

Although every effort has been made to ensure that website addresses are correct at time of going to press, Hodder Gibson cannot be held responsible for the content of any website mentioned in this book. It is sometimes possible to find a relocated web page by typing in the address of the home page for a website in the URL window of your browser.

Hachette UK's policy is to use papers that are natural, renewable and recyclable products and made from wood grown in well-managed forests and other controlled sources. The logging and manufacturing processes are expected to conform to the environmental regulations of the country of origin.

Orders: please contact Bookpoint Ltd, 130 Park Drive, Milton Park, Abingdon, Oxon OX14 4SE. Telephone: (44) 01235 827827. Fax: (44) 01235 400454. Email: education@bookpoint.co.uk. Lines are open from 9 a.m. to 5 p.m., Monday to Saturday, with a 24-hour message answering service. Visit our website at www.hoddereducation.co.uk. Hodder Gibson can also be contacted directly at hoddergibson@hodder.co.uk

Contents

Introduction

This revision book will help you to achieve the best possible result in your Higher Modern Studies examination by explaining clearly what you need to know about the exam and what knowledge and skills you will need to display.

Access to the Hodder Gibson *Higher Modern Studies* textbooks will enhance the use of this revision guide.

The textbooks are:
- *Democracy in Scotland and the UK*
- *Social Issues in the UK*
- *International Issues.*

You have already covered all or most of the skills and knowledge required to pass the exam but revision has a very important role to play. By working your way through this book you will find it much easier to understand what you need to display in your assessment answers. This will enhance your confidence and enable you to achieve your full potential.

You will also find advice about the assignment, in which you will apply research and decision-making skills in the context of a Modern Studies topic or issue of your own choice. This assignment is important as it will be marked by SQA and will contribute to your overall mark and grade.

We hope you will find this book of great value and support.

Good luck!

How you will be tested

You will have studied the following three sections:
- Democracy in Scotland and the United Kingdom
- Social Issues in the United Kingdom
- International Issues.

The Higher award is made up of two externally marked assessments:
- Higher question paper 1 and paper 2 (80 marks)
  - Paper 1 is allocated 52 marks and you will have 1 hour and 45 minutes to complete it
  - Paper 2 is allocated 28 marks and you will have 1 hour and 15 minutes to complete it
- Higher assignment (30 marks). You will have 1 hour and 30 minutes to complete it.

The marks you achieve in the question papers and assignment are added together and an overall mark will indicate a pass or fail. From this, your course award will then be graded.

Part One: Assessment

Chapter 1

The exam

The question papers

Question paper 1 has three sections:

- Section 1: Democracy in Scotland and the UK
  You will answer one essay from a choice of **three**.
- Section 2: Social Issues in the UK
  You will answer one essay from a choice of **two** from your chosen study.
- Section 3: International Issues
  You will answer one essay from a choice of **two** from your chosen study.

You will have 1 hour and 45 minutes to answer two 20-mark questions and one 12-mark question.

Question paper 2 has three mandatory questions as outlined below.

You will have 1 hour and 15 minutes to answer two 10-mark questions and one 8-mark question.

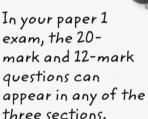

Remember

In your paper 1 exam, the 20-mark and 12-mark questions can appear in any of the three sections.

What types of questions will I need to answer?

There are three types of skills questions that you will have practised in class. These are:

1 Using between two and four sources of information **to detect and explain the degree of objectivity of a given statement (10 marks)**.
2 Using between two and four sources of information **to identify what conclusions can be drawn (10 marks)**.
3 Using sources of information **to evaluate their reliability (8 marks)**.

In Part Five of this book we will look at examples of skills-based questions and students' answers.

In the knowledge section of your exam you will answer four types of questions:

- **Analyse: 12-mark extended response**, for example:
  Analyse the new powers granted to the Scottish Parliament by the UK Government in recent years.
- **Evaluate: 12-mark extended response**, for example:
  Evaluate the effectiveness of government policies in reducing social and economic inequality experienced by a group in society.

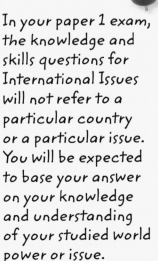

Remember

In your paper 1 exam, the knowledge and skills questions for International Issues will not refer to a particular country or a particular issue. You will be expected to base your answer on your knowledge and understanding of your studied world power or issue.

- **Discuss: 20-mark extended response**, for example:
  With reference to a world power you have studied:
  The political system of this country effectively protects the rights of its citizens.
  Discuss.
- **To what extent: 20-mark extended response**, for example:
  With reference to a world issue you have studied:
  To what extent have international organisations been effective in addressing this issue?

Do I have a choice?

Your teacher will usually have chosen one topic from each of the three sections for you to study and you will answer questions on these topics in your exam. In Democracy in Scotland and the UK there will be a mandatory (compulsory) section covering Scotland's place in the UK political system and usually you will then concentrate on either the UK or the Scottish dimension. Your teacher will choose from the options listed below for each section.

Section of the course	Option one	Option two
Democracy in Scotland and the UK	Democracy in Scotland	Democracy in the UK
Social Issues in the UK	Social Inequality	Crime and the Law
International Issues	World Powers	World Issues

Hints & tips ★

What makes a good knowledge answer?

✓ One that answers the question and only provides knowledge and understanding and analysis/evaluation that is **relevant** to the question.

✓ One that is an **appropriate length**. Use the number of marks assigned to each question as a guide to how much you should write and how much time to devote to the question. An answer to a 20-mark extended writing question should include greater higher-order skills of analysis and evaluation and a more structured answer than one to a 12-mark question.

✓ One that uses **up-to-date** examples to illustrate your understanding of the question being asked.

✓ One that includes a **range** of points, detailed explanation and description and accurate exemplification, analysis and evaluation.

What makes a bad knowledge answer?

✓ One that does not answer the question, or tries to change the question being asked. This is sometimes called 'turning a question'.

✓ One that gives detailed description or explanation that is not relevant to the question.

✓ One that contains information that is out of date (you should be especially careful of this in the International Issues section).

✓ One that simply consists of a list of facts with no development. You must tailor your answer to the question, and only give information that is relevant to what is being asked.

Chapter 2

The assignment

Before your exam in May, you will carry out the assignment as part of your Higher course assessment. Your teacher will probably plan to complete this during the spring term before you sit the exam.

What is the assignment?

The assignment will apply research and decision-making skills in the context of a Modern Studies issue. You can choose a political, social or international issue. The information collected should display knowledge and understanding of the topic or issue chosen. SQA recommend that you should devote about eight hours for the research stage, including preparation time for the production of evidence.

The results of the research will be written up under controlled assessment conditions and must be completed within one hour and 30 minutes. The assignment is very important as it is worth a total of 30 marks.

You are allowed to bring two single-sided sheets of A4 paper (containing your research evidence) into the exam to refer to during the write-up. This is referred to as 'research evidence' and consists of materials collected during the research stage of the assignment.

What type of issue should I choose?

With agreement from your teacher, you should choose a topic that enables you to make a decision about an issue, for example: 'The voting age in all Scottish and UK elections should be reduced to sixteen.'

Where do I gather information from?

The information gathered for your research can be broken down into two parts: *primary information* and *secondary information*.

Primary information

Primary information is evidence that you have gathered by yourself and is unique to your personal research. The ways in which you gather primary evidence can vary greatly – some examples are given below:

- surveys/questionnaires
- interviews
- emails
- letters
- focus groups
- field study.

Secondary information

Secondary information is evidence that you have gathered from research that was carried out by others. You should use it to help support your personal research. There are vast amounts of secondary information available, in many different formats – just a few examples are below:

- school textbooks, newspapers and magazines
- internet search engines and websites
- TV and radio programmes
- mobile phone apps
- social media such as Twitter
- library books and articles.

How do I plan my research?

To carry out a successful piece of personal research, you need to plan it effectively. You will need to keep all evidence of your planning so that your work can be accurately marked.

You may wish to consider the following questions about your primary and secondary sources:

- What useful information have I gained from this source to help me research my issue?
- How reliable is the information gathered from the source?
- Could the source contain bias or exaggeration?

How is the assignment marked?

The allocation of marks is based on the following criteria:

1   Identifying and displaying knowledge and understanding of the issue about which a decision is to be made, including alternative courses of action – up to a maximum of **10 marks**.
    You should agree an issue to research with your teacher. It has to relate to one or more of the issues that you study in your course:
    - Democracy in Scotland and the United Kingdom
    - Social Issues in the United Kingdom
    - International Issues.

2   Synthesising and analysing information from a range of sources, including use of specified resources – up to a maximum of **10 marks**. You will research a wide range of sources to provide contrasting views on your chosen issue. By linking information from a variety of sources and viewpoints, you will be able to enrich and synthesise the arguments that are developed in your report.

3   Evaluating the usefulness and reliability of a range of sources of information – up to a maximum of **2 marks**. To achieve 2 marks, a comparative judgement of the sources must be made.
    You will comment on the background and nature of the source. Does it provide only one point of view? Are its findings up to date, and so are its comments still relevant today?

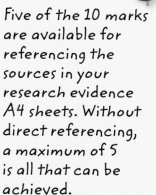

Remember

Five of the 10 marks are available for referencing the sources in your research evidence A4 sheets. Without direct referencing, a maximum of 5 is all that can be achieved.

4   Communicating information using the convention of a report – up to a maximum of **4 marks**.
    Remember that you are not writing an essay; you are considering the arguments for and against a proposal. You should write in the form of a report and include subheadings.
    Here you should make conclusions relevant to the research issue.
    Try to avoid repeating findings you have already given.
5   Reaching a decision, supported by evidence, about the issue – up to a maximum of **4 marks**.
    The decision should be based on the body of evidence you have provided in the report.

See Part Five (page 131) for advice on the best way to unlock the marks of the assignment and worked examples.

Remember

The write-up of your research must be in the form of a report. You can include a summary of your findings in your notes that you bring into the exam as you must refer to these findings in your write-up, but you cannot simply copy them out.

Part Two: Democracy in Scotland and the UK

This section of the book provides summary course notes for the Democracy in Scotland and the UK area of study.

You will have studied the compulsory features of this section and you will have concentrated on either:

- the UK Executive and parliamentary representatives or
- the Scottish Executive and parliamentary representatives.

In the extended response/essay section of the exam, you will answer either a 12-mark question or a 20-mark question.

Figure 3.1 The UK and Scottish Parliament buildings

Chapter 3

UK constitutional arrangements and voting systems

What you should know

SQA requirements

To be successful in this section, you should know about:

★ the constitutional arrangements of the UK, including the Scottish Parliament and other devolved bodies
★ the possible alternatives for the governance of Scotland
★ the implications of the UK's decision to leave the European Union (EU)
★ the strengths and weaknesses of different electoral systems used in elections within the UK
★ the factors which influence voting behaviour including class, age and media.

UK constitutional arrangements

The UK is a parliamentary democracy with a constitutional monarch who has effectively no political power. The **royal prerogatives** held by the monarch, such as the power to dissolve parliament, are in actual fact held by the prime minister, who is in turn responsible to an elected House of Commons. The Queen is the head of state to the people of England, Scotland, Northern Ireland and Wales and to the peoples of the 15 realms of the Commonwealth. Figure 3.2 below illustrates the political system of the UK. Parliamentary sovereignty ensures all powers are vested in the UK Parliament and the powers granted to the **devolved** governments can be returned to the UK Parliament and the devolved parliaments abolished.

Key terms

Royal prerogatives: Powers of the monarch that are exercised in the crown's name by the prime minister and government ministers.

Devolved: Powers that have been transferred from central government to local or regional administration.

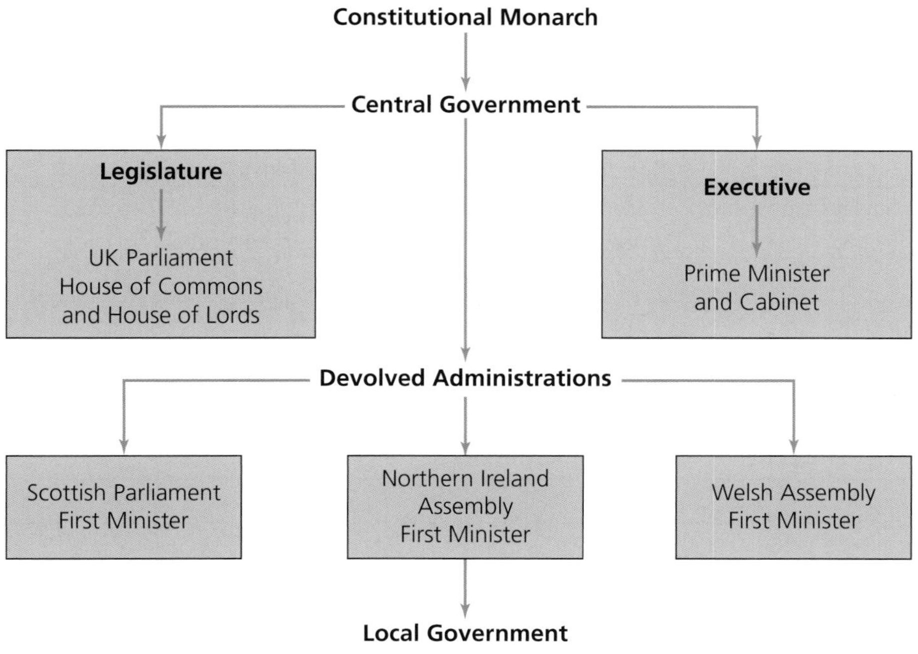

```
                    Constitutional Monarch
                            │
                            ▼
                   Central Government
          ┌─────────────────┼─────────────────┐
          ▼                                     ▼
      Legislature                           Executive

    UK Parliament                         Prime Minister
   House of Commons                        and Cabinet
  and House of Lords

          └─────────────────┼─────────────────┐
                            ▼
                 Devolved Administrations
          ┌─────────────────┼─────────────────┐
          ▼                  ▼                  ▼
  Scottish Parliament   Northern Ireland    Welsh Assembly
   First Minister         Assembly          First Minister
                        First Minister
                            │
                            ▼
                    Local Government
```

Figure 3.2 The structure of the UK political system

The UK central government has responsibility for national affairs, such as the economy, defence, foreign policy and the environment. In the UK, the prime minister leads the government with the support of the cabinet and ministers. Departments and their agencies are responsible for putting government policy into practice.

The role and powers of the devolved bodies

In Northern Ireland, Scotland and Wales, some government policies and public services are different from those in England. The UK central government has given certain powers to devolved governments, so that they can make decisions for their own areas. The Scottish Parliament, the National Assembly for Wales and the Northern Ireland Assembly were established and took control in 1999. The arrangements are different for each, reflecting their history and administrative structures. The UK Government remains responsible for national policy on all matters that have not been devolved, including foreign affairs, defence, trade and aspects of social security (see Table 3.1).

In recent years further important powers have been granted to the Scottish Parliament (see page 12).

Table 3.1 Reserved issues and devolved powers granted in 1999

Reserved issues	Devolved powers	
Constitutional matters	Education and training	
UK foreign policy	Health	
UK defence and national security	Local government	
Fiscal, economic and monetary system	Social work	
Immigration and nationality	Housing	
Energy: electricity, coal, gas and nuclear energy	Planning	
Common markets	Tourism, economic development and financial assistance to industry	
Trade and industry, including competition and customer protection	Law and home affairs, including most aspects of criminal and civil law, the prosecution system and the courts	
Some aspects of transport, including railways, transport safety and regulation	Some aspects of transport, including the Scottish road network, bus policy and ports and harbours	
Employment legislation	Police and fire services	
Social security	The environment	
Gambling and the National Lottery	Natural and built heritage	
Data protection	Agriculture, forestry and fishing	
Abortion, human fertilisation, embryology and genetics	Sport and the arts	
Equal opportunities		

Scottish Parliament

The Scottish Parliament debates topical issues and passes laws on devolved matters that affect Scotland. It also scrutinises the work and policies of the Scottish Government. It is made up of 129 elected Members of the Scottish Parliament (MSPs) and meets at Holyrood in Edinburgh. Since 1999, the Scottish Parliament has held responsibility for the powers devolved to Scotland. These original devolved powers, such as education, are listed in Table 3.1. More powers continue to be devolved to Scotland. As part of the 2012 Scotland Act, MSPs at Holyrood became responsible for the licence of air guns and drink-driving limits (which came into force in December 2014). However, the SNP and members of the general public believed that Holyrood should hold even more powers referred to as 'devo-max'.

Welsh Assembly

The National Assembly for Wales is the representative body that holds law-making powers on devolved matters. It debates and approves legislation. The role of the Assembly is to scrutinise and monitor the Welsh Assembly Government. It has 60 elected members and meets in the Senedd.

Northern Ireland Assembly

The Northern Ireland Assembly was established as a result of the Belfast Agreement (also known as the Good Friday Agreement) in 1998. Devolution to Northern Ireland was suspended in October 2002 and restored on 8 May 2007.

Possible alternatives for the governance of Scotland

The two main alternatives are an independent Scotland with full **sovereignty** or a Scotland with limited devolved powers but remaining as an integral part of the United Kingdom. All of the main UK parties support the union. However, during the 2014 **referendum**, with the possibility of a Yes independence vote, 'The Vow' was made by the three UK leaders to grant more extensive powers, referred to as 'devo-max', if Scotland voted to remain in the union.

It was hoped that this concession would sway voters who were unhappy with the limited powers of the Scottish Parliament not to vote for independence. According to Alex Salmond, 'The Vow' was a key reason why the Scottish people did not vote for independence.

Key terms

Sovereignty: Supreme power.
Referendum: The electorate, not their representatives, vote to accept or reject a proposal.

The Scottish referendum, September 2014

After winning an overall majority in the 2011 Scottish Parliament elections, the SNP's bill to hold a referendum on independence was passed by the Scottish Parliament. Prime Minister David Cameron gave Westminster's permission for a referendum to be held on 18 September 2014. In a long campaign, two main groups were formed: the independence group – Yes Scotland – and the 'remain in UK' group – Better Together (see box). Table 3.2 highlights the key arguments used in 2014.

Yes Scotland

- Led by Alex Salmond and supported by the SNP, Scottish Greens and Scottish Socialists
- Strong grassroots support with over 300 local groups active in their communities
- A positive campaign that energised the political involvement of ordinary Scots but was weak on the currency of an independent Scotland

Better Together

- Led by Labour's Alistair Darling and supported by Scottish Labour, Scottish Conservative and Scottish Liberal Democrats
- Strong UK support from their UK-based parties
- A negative campaign, referred to as 'Project Fear' by Yes Scotland supporters (Scottish Labour were to pay a high price for working in partnership with the Conservatives when they lost 40 of their 41 Scottish MPs at the 2015 general election)

Figure 3.3 The Yes Scotland and Better Together campaigns

Table 3.2 Key points for and against independence in 2014

For	Against
National debt	
Alex Salmond stressed that Scotland would have been committed to honouring its share of the UK national debt but only if given a share of the assets, including the pound.	Alistair Darling maintained that a currency union would not be possible in the event of independence and Scotland could not demand 'the best of both worlds'.
The NHS	
Sir Harry Burns, former Chief Medical Officer for Scotland, announced the week before the referendum that an independent Scotland was necessary to secure the future of the NHS, as NHS cuts, charging and privatisation become an ever-increasing aspect of the NHS.	Better Together argued that as health is a devolved issue, Scotland will always be able to protect the NHS from privatisation. They argued that the Nationalists were scaremongering to win votes. ⇨

Oil	
Alex Salmond argued that about £1 billion – one-tenth of the oil revenues – could have formed an oil fund similar to the one operated in Norway. Yes Scotland was convinced that Scottish oil estimates were accurate and that the revenue created would contribute to Scotland's success as an independent country.	Opponents of Scottish independence argued that Yes Scotland overestimated the wealth that could be created by North Sea oil. Sir Ian Wood, the oil billionaire, warned that the Yes Scotland campaign was wrong to say that 24 billion barrels are left and the figure is more likely to be 15–16 billion barrels.
Currency	
The Scottish Government argued that it would be in the best interests of both an independent Scotland and the rest of the UK for Scotland to share the pound and retain the Bank of England as a lender of last resorts to bail out Scottish-based banks if needed. They pointed to the case of Belgium and Luxembourg, who have successfully been in a currency union for decades.	The UK **Coalition Government**, along with the Labour Party, ruled out the possibility of a currency union with Scotland. Instead, they suggested that Scotland could either use the pound in the same way that Panama uses the US dollar, set up a new currency or use the euro.
The European Union	
Nationalists argued that Scotland would not have to reapply to join the EU as citizens would continue to be EU citizens after a period of negotiation of Scotland's new terms.	Unionists argued that if Scotland had voted to leave the UK, it would have voted to leave an EU member state and would therefore have to reapply as a new member state, relying on the support of governments such as Spain, which would not support such an application.
Nuclear weapons/defence	
Yes Scotland argued that an independent Scotland would be free from nuclear weapons, which are currently stored on the Clyde. They also argued that Scotland would join NATO but focus a new Scottish army's effort on humanitarian work.	It was argued that storage of nuclear weapons on the Clyde provided jobs for people in the local community and that in the event of a Yes vote it would be extremely expensive for these to be relocated. Better Together also argued that a nuclear-free Scotland would not be granted NATO membership.

> **Key term**
>
> **Coalition government:** When two or more political parties form a government.

Result of the 2014 Scottish Independence referendum

The Scottish people decided to remain in the union rather than face the uncertainties of an independent Scotland outside the EU (see Table 3.3). It was clear that those who lived in wealthier areas were more likely to vote No and the poorest in society were more likely to vote Yes.

Table 3.3 Should Scotland be an independent country?

	Votes	%
Yes	1,617,989	44.7
No	2,001,926	55.3

Fact file

- There was a massive turnout of 85 per cent of the Scottish electorate.
- The four local councils with the highest Yes votes – Dundee, Glasgow, North Lanarkshire and West Dunbartonshire – have high rates of deprivation.
- The Yes vote for men was 49 per cent but only 43 per cent for women.
- Alex Salmond immediately resigned from his post of first minister and leader of the SNP and was replaced by Nicola Sturgeon.
- In 2016 the Scotland Act received the royal assent and Scotland received some of the powers promised in 'The Vow'. All of the SNP amendments for greater powers were rejected by the Conservative Government.

Powers granted to the Scottish Parliament under the 2012 and 2016 Scotland Acts (Devo-max)

- Control over licences for air guns and stamp duty (tax paid on buying a house)
- Control over drink-driving limits – now much more severe than the rest of the UK
- Control over tax rates in Scotland – in April 2016 tax rates were set in Scotland at a different rate from the rest of the UK (see new tax rates on page 53)
- Control over abortion laws
- Some welfare powers such as Winter Fuel Payments and Disability Living Allowance (see the new welfare powers on page 52).

A second Scottish referendum?

- In the June 2016 EU referendum, a relatively narrow majority of UK citizens voted to leave the EU. In contrast, over 60 per cent of the Scottish public voted to remain in the EU. This has led to a demand for a new Scottish referendum.
- The UK Government has refused to return key powers that reside with the EU to the Scottish Government once the UK leaves. Although the Scottish Parliament refused to give consent to this 'power grab' in areas such as agriculture and fishing, the UK Parliament ignored their objections. The UK Government argues that all powers granted to the Scottish Parliament are at their discretion and can be removed.
- A No **Brexit** deal is now a strong possibility and would probably damage the Scottish economy. Nicola Sturgeon is being urged to put forward legislation for a second referendum. (This would require the consent of the UK Government.)

Key terms

Brexit and Brexiteers: Terms given to the process of leaving the EU and to those who supported Brexit.

Possible implications of the UK leaving the EU

In order to end internal conflict within the Conservative Party and defections to UKIP, Prime Minister David Cameron promised to hold a referendum on whether 'the UK should remain a member of the European Union or leave the European Union'. Those in favour of leaving argued that it would restore UK sovereignty and give the UK back control of its own borders. Those not in favour argued that leaving would damage the UK economy and the UK's international influence. The referendum was held on 23 June 2016 and the result was a narrow victory for leaving the EU. England and Wales voted to leave but Scotland and Northern Ireland did not (see Table 3.4).

Table 3.4 June 2016 EU referendum results across the UK

The UK and its nations	Remain	Leave
UK	48.1	51.9
England	46.6	53.4
Northern Ireland	55.8	44.2
Scotland	62.0	38.0
Wales	47.5	52.5

Table 3.5 The benefits and drawbacks of Brexit

Benefits	Drawbacks
Money will be saved on membership fees. In 2016, Britain paid £13.1 billion to the EU.	There will be a loss of EU investment in the UK. In 2016, the UK received £4.5 billion worth of spending.
The UK will be free to establish its own trade deals.	It will be more difficult to trade with EU member countries.
The UK Government will be able to set its own immigration laws.	There will be an impact on services such as health, agriculture and tourism which depend heavily on EU workers.
Jobs now being done by EU citizens will be open to British citizens.	It will be more difficult for British workers to seek employment in the EU. Also, many of the jobs currently being done by EU citizens are unattractive to British workers.
There will be an opportunity to re-establish Britain as an independent nation with global connections.	The UK will lose its influence in Europe and in international bodies.
Britain will be able to regain control in areas such as fishing rights.	Britain will have limited access (if any) to the single market.
There will be greater freedom to check and control who crosses the UK border.	Britain will lose the collective support of the EU in security matters.
The democratic rights of the citizens of the UK who voted to leave will be honoured.	Scotland voted decisively to remain as did Northern Ireland, so the wishes of the voters in those areas have been ignored.
The UK Parliament will regain sovereignty.	The issue of Northern Ireland had originally been ignored.

Key events: the road to Brexit

- **23 January 2013** – Prime Minister David Cameron says he is in favour of an in/out referendum on the UK's membership of the EU.
- **7 May 2015** – In the general election, David Cameron wins a twelve-seat majority with a manifesto that includes the commitment to hold an in/out referendum.
- **23 June 2016** – The referendum sees Leave campaigners win a narrow victory with 51.9% voting to leave the EU and 48.1% voting to remain in the EU. Mr Cameron resigns immediately as prime minister.
- **13 July 2016** – Theresa May becomes prime minister.
- **29 March 2017** – She triggers Article 50, which starts the clock on the process of the UK leaving the EU.
- **8 June 2017** – After calling a snap election, Theresa May loses her majority in Parliament. Northern Ireland's DUP – led by Arlene Foster – makes a deal with the Conservatives and its votes allow Theresa May to stay in power.
- **26 June 2017** – Formal negotiations on withdrawal begin between the UK and the EU.
- **13 December 2017** – Rebel Tory MPs side with the Opposition, forcing the Government to guarantee a vote on the final Brexit deal, when it has been struck with Brussels.
- **15 December 2017** – The EU agrees to move on to the second phase of negotiations after an agreement is reached on the Brexit 'divorce bill', Irish border and EU citizens' rights.
- **19 March 2018** – The UK and EU make decisive steps in negotiations, including agreements on dates for a transitional period after Brexit day, the status of EU citizens in the UK before and after that time and the fishing policy. Issues still to be resolved include the Northern Ireland border.
- **31 October 2018** – MPs will get to vote on the final deal in the UK Parliament before 29 March 2019.
- **29 March 2019: Brexit day** – The UK ends its membership of the European Union at 23:00 GMT and enters a transition period.
- **31 December 2020** – The transition period is due to end and the new economic and political relationship between the UK and the EU will begin.

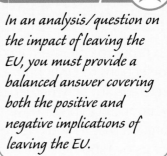

Hints & tips

In an analysis/question on the impact of leaving the EU, you must provide a balanced answer covering both the positive and negative implications of leaving the EU.

Electoral systems and voting behaviour

UK general elections are held every five years. In UK elections, the electoral system used is known as First Past The Post (FPTP). In 2011, a referendum was held on replacing FPTP with the Alternative Vote (AV) – a modified version of FPTP. However, on a low turnout voters rejected AV. In Scotland elections take place every four years. In Scottish parliamentary elections and local council elections Proportional Representation (PR) is used. For Scottish Parliament elections the PR system used is called the Additional Member System (AMS). For Scottish local council elections the Single Transferable Vote (STV) is used. Party List (PL) is the type of PR used in European elections.

First Past The Post

First Past The Post (FPTP) is the electoral system used in UK general elections. It is a simple majority system whereby in each of the UK's 650 constituencies the candidate with the most votes wins the seat and becomes the MP in that constituency.

Table 3.6 Arguments for and against FPTP

Arguments for FPTP	Arguments against FPTP
FPTP is easy to understand – a particular benefit for elderly and first-time voters.	FPTP does not produce a proportional result. This means that the percentage of votes received using FPTP does not compare with the percentage of seats gained. This is unfair and means that winners are over-represented. In 2015, the Conservatives gained 50.9 per cent of the seats in Westminster with only 36.9 per cent of the votes.
The voter simply has to mark an X next to the candidate of their choice on the ballot paper and the candidate who receives the most votes in that constituency wins the seat in parliament. The result of this simple and easy-to-understand system is that it will often encourage voter turnout. In 2015, 66 per cent of people turned out to vote in the general election, compared to 56 per cent of voters for the more complicated Scottish election using AMS (2016).	It can result in a lot of wasted votes. As it is the person with the most votes who wins the constituency, all the other votes are discounted and individuals do not have their votes heard. This can result in **voter apathy** as voters feel that their votes do not count.
The results of the elections are produced very quickly. The votes are counted for each of the candidates in a constituency and whoever gets the most wins. This is a reasonably quick process and consequently the result of the election is announced the next day. In 2015 in Houghton, Sunderland, the winning candidate was announced only 48 minutes after the polling stations were closed.	FPTP is unfair to smaller parties. Smaller parties that only get a low percentage of votes will gain no representation because they do not win in any constituency. In 2015, UKIP had only one MP in the House of Commons despite gaining 3.9 million votes.
Traditionally FPTP has been relied upon to produce a clear winner, which avoids minority governments or coalitions. The 2010 general election did, however, produce a coalition government between the Conservatives and the Liberal Democrats. This was the first time that the winning party did not have an overall majority since 1974. Once again, in 2017, FPTP failed to elect a majority government as the Conservatives formed a minority government with 48.9% of the vote.	FPTP favours larger parties. The bigger parties are more likely to win in constituencies and gain more MPs. As the number of votes across all constituencies is not added up, this favours the larger parties. Since 1945, with the exception of the governments formed in 2010 and 2017, all governments in the UK have either been Labour or Conservative.
FPTP retains a strong MP–constituency link. The electorate votes directly for an MP and once the MP is elected the constituents are fully aware of who they are and can hold them accountable for their actions. In contrast, under Proportional Representation systems, more than one representative can be elected.	The winning MP may not have a majority of the votes cast; in 1992, a Liberal Democrat candidate won with only 26 per cent of the vote.

Additional Member System

The Scottish Parliament, Welsh Assembly and London Assembly are all elected using the Additional Member System (AMS). This system is a mixture of First Past The Post and Proportional Representation (PR). In Scotland, voters cast two votes. The first vote is used to elect the 73 constituency MSPs. The second vote uses the Party List system of PR. In this vote, the electorate choose between parties who will represent them in their region. There are eight regions and each region elects seven MSPs, making the total number of MSPs 129.

Key term

Voter apathy: A lack of interest or engagement in the political process.

Table 3.7 Arguments for and against AMS

Arguments for AMS	Arguments against AMS
As there are two ballot papers, AMS is more proportional. One uses FPTP and the other uses the Party/Regional List. In 2016, the SNP won 46.5 per cent of the vote in the Scottish Parliament election and this translated into 63 seats, or 48.8 per cent of the seats available – a far more proportional outcome than FPTP would allow.	AMS is more complicated for voters to understand as it features two votes, and this can confuse some voters who are used to voting using FPTP in British elections. In the 2007 Scottish Parliament elections, a staggering 140,000 ballot papers were rejected.
AMS usually creates coalition governments. This is seen as an advantage because one party cannot force opinions upon the people, especially when they do not have more than 50 per cent of the vote. This is an advantage of AMS because coalitions can create consensus and agreement on policies. The 1999 and 2003 Scottish elections created coalition governments that passed many important laws in Scotland, such as the smoking ban. Despite winning the first majority government in 2011, the SNP formed a minority government in 2016.	AMS often creates coalition governments. Although this is sometimes regarded as a strength of the system, it can also be deemed a weakness. The electorate never votes for a coalition government on their ballot paper. This means that they are not democratic. No one voted for the coalition between Labour and Liberal Democrats in Scotland from 1999 to 2007. Again, the SNP minority Government of 2007–2011 failed to get through some of its key policies, such as minimum pricing of alcohol.
AMS allows for greater voter choice as there are two votes. In the first vote, one MSP is elected per constituency. In the second vote, cast using PR, seven MSPs are elected to each region. Voters in Glasgow Kelvin can vote for a constituency candidate like Sandra White of the SNP, but could vote for a totally different party, such as the Green Party, in the second regional vote. Therefore the electorate has more choice.	It can often be the case that smaller parties achieve too much power in AMS. AMS allows parties that have very little support to be involved in coalition governments, or influence minority governments, which can mean they have a say in decisions made and laws passed. In 2017 and 2018, the Scottish Greens 'persuaded' the SNP minority government to change its budget proposals in return for their support in passing the budget.
AMS is fairer on smaller parties as it enables them to gain a percentage of seats equal to the percentage of votes they have gained by using PR in the second vote. The Green Party gained seats in the Scottish Parliament election despite never gaining any under FPTP.	The regional MSPs elected through the PR vote in AMS are not directly voted for by the people. The people vote for a party and the party decides which candidates will become MSPs. Also, very few people can hold them accountable for their actions as they do not know who they are.

Single Transferable Vote

The Single Transferable Vote (STV) was first used in Scottish local elections in May 2007. Voters rank the candidates in order of preference and can vote for as few or as many candidates as they like. A quota system is then used to calculate the minimum number of votes required to win a seat.

Table 3.8 Arguments for and against STV

Arguments for STV	Arguments against STV
The STV system is more proportional as candidates must reach a certain 'quota' of votes to be elected, with all votes being counted and affecting the result. Therefore the percentage of votes is closer to the percentage of seats. In the 2007 Scottish Local Authority Elections, the SNP gained roughly the same percentage of seats within wards as they did votes, and big parties like Labour lost out.	STV is thought to be more confusing than many other electoral systems. The STV system means that people are asked to cast their vote more than once on the same ballot paper. This can confuse some voters who are used to voting using FPTP in British elections. Therefore it may discourage people from voting. Notoriously, in the 2007 Scottish Local Authority Elections, 100,000 people 'spoilt' their votes as they were confused about the voting system. These votes were not counted. Furthermore, voter turnout was only 32 per cent in some areas of Scotland.

⇒

Arguments for STV	Arguments against STV
STV is fairer to smaller parties and gives them a better chance of gaining seats. This means that STV allows small parties to gain a percentage of votes that matches the percentage of seats they have gained as it is a Proportional Representation system. Therefore smaller parties gain a larger percentage of support. In 2017, the Scottish Green Party won 19 seats, five more than in 2012.	STV can often produce results to which no one agreed. STV produces a result that means many local authorities have no party with overall control. Therefore it is hard to make decisions and often parties need to form coalitions at local level to be able to make decisions. No one actually voted for this and it can be seen as undemocratic. In 2017, no council in mainland Scotland had overall control. There is a danger that this will cause slow policy-making and indecision, as was seen in the case of the Edinburgh tram system.
There are usually fewer wasted votes in STV. The voters must place candidates in order of preference; they can place as many or as few votes as they wish. As candidates must reach a certain 'quota' of votes then every vote cast must be counted.	STV can allow more power to fall into the hands of smaller parties. STV allows parties that have very little support to be involved in coalition agreements, which can mean they have a say in decisions.
STV allows more choice for the electorate. Voters can vote for as many or as few candidates as they wish. Therefore there is more choice about who they can vote for in terms of parties and candidates.	The results from STV take longer than other systems. The public is asked to vote for more than one candidate, and they can often cast up to as many as seven votes. Also the 'quota' can only be decided when the votes are all cast. Once this has happened the votes must be counted and then re-counted until a winner can be declared.

National/regional party list

This PL system was introduced for elections to the European Parliament in 1999. Each party draws up a list of candidates ranked according to the party's preference, with the more important candidates ranked at the top of the list. Electors then vote for a party rather than a person. Representatives are elected from 11 large multi-member regions, each electing between three and ten MEPs. In the 2014 European Elections, Scotland elected six MEPs.

Summary of the 2014 European elections

The 2014 European Elections were dominated by anti-establishment parties. There was a trend across Europe against pro-federalist politicians and towards Eurosceptic parties, with the largest federalist Alliance (the European People's Party) losing 6 per cent of the Parliament. Although Eurosceptic Alliances increased their representation, they are still in the minority with approximately 25 per cent of seats.

In the UK 2014 European Elections, the UK Independence Party (UKIP) won with 27.5 per cent of the popular vote, against Labour (25.4 per cent) and Conservative (23.9 per cent). It was the first time since 1906 that a party other than Labour or the Conservatives had won a national election. In Scotland, UKIP won one of the six Scottish European seats, with the Liberal Democrats losing their only seat.

Table 3.9 Arguments for and against Party List (PL)

Arguments for PL	Arguments against PL
As party lists are a form of PR they enjoy the benefit of being proportional and every vote has an equal value.	The MP–constituent link is weaker as there is no one representative.
PL is a simple system for voters to use. The party selects the candidates who will appear on their list and the electorate simply votes for a political party. If a party gains 30 per cent of the vote, the top 30 per cent of their candidates will be elected.	Voters have no choice over the candidate elected as they only vote for a party, with the party leaders choosing the candidate.
It can help to ensure fairer representation of groups that are normally under-represented in the political system. Parties can put female and ethnic minority candidates at the top of their lists, increasing the likelihood that they will be elected.	PL can lead to under-representation as party leaders may choose people similar to them to stand, rather than candidates from under-represented groups such as women and ethnic minorities.
PL traditionally creates coalition governments and this results in a broader range of parties being represented.	The creation of coalitions can also be seen as a weakness of the PL system.
	As in other forms of PR, the balance of power can lie with smaller parties, which can be undemocratic.

Voting behaviour

Main factors that affect voting behaviour

There are several factors that affect voting behaviour. Some are short-term factors such as the media, party image, leadership style and policy issues, while others are long-term factors such as social class, age, gender, ethnicity and religion.

Long-term factors

Social class

From 1945 to 1970, there was a clear link between a person's voting behaviour and their class. During this time, 65 per cent of working-class people voted for Labour, while 85 per cent of the middle class voted for the Conservatives. However, there were always working-class people who voted Conservative and middle-class Labour voters. Since 1970, as a result of **class de-alignment**, there has been a decline in the importance of class as the main determinant of voting behaviour. More recent general elections have provided evidence that social class is no longer so important in shaping political attitudes. In 1974, Labour won 57 per cent of working-class votes, but by the 2017 general election this had fallen to 40 per cent. The Conservative Party in 1974 won 56 per cent of the middle-class vote, but this had fallen to 43 per cent in 2015.

> **Key term**
>
> **Class de-alignment:** When voters no longer align themselves with a particular political party on the basis of their social class.

Age

A person's age is another factor that influences voting behaviour as it not only determines who a person votes for but also if they will vote at all. Young voters outside Scotland will traditionally vote Labour, while older voters vote Conservative. This may be partly due to the perception that the Conservative Party will favour more traditional values. Furthermore, in the 2015 UK general election, voting was much higher in the elderly group (65 and over), where older voters were more likely to vote than 18- to

26-year-olds, at 78 per cent versus 44 per cent. Age was also a significant factor in determining voting behaviour in the 2016 European Union referendum. Over-65s were more than twice as likely as under-25s to have voted to leave the European Union. While 29 per cent of under-25s voted to leave, this figure was 64 per cent among over-65s. In the 2017 general election, young people in England and Wales overwhelmingly voted Labour; Corbyn had promised free university tuition. According to John Curtice of the National Centre for Social Research, Labour won 43 of the 60 constituencies where full-time students made up 15 per cent or more of the adult population. Significantly, according to the post-election survey by YouGov, turnout among those aged 18–19 was 57 per cent and 20–24 was 59 per cent, far higher than the 2015 turnout.

Gender

Gender also affects voting behaviour. Women have historically been far more likely to vote for the Conservatives and to make up the majority of Tory voters. However, there have been recent changes and, in particular, the 1997 election was significant because New Labour overcame this gender gap through their female-friendly policies. As a result, there were more women candidates and 101 female Labour MPs were elected. Women who become more middle class and are better educated are more likely to move to the left. In recent elections, the gap between men and women has been small with an equal split between Conservatives and Labour among female voters. Men are slightly more likely to vote for the Tories (45 per cent in the 2017 general election).

Ethnicity

Ethnicity is also an important factor in determining a person's voting behaviour. Recent years' election results indicate that black and Asian voters are more likely to vote for Labour, but it is also possible that this can be attributed to their social class. Traditionally, many people from ethnic minorities in Britain are from lower socio-economic groups, which have typically tended to be Labour voters. However, there are also many affluent black and Asian voters who do not identify with Labour. In the 2017 general election, an estimated 65 per cent of ethnic minorities voted for Labour. Despite being ridiculed by the press in the run-up to the election, Labour politician Diane Abbott secured a majority of over 35,000 in Hackney and Stoke Newington (it has been argued in some quarters that this was largely due to the power of the ethnic minority vote as the constituency is home to a 42 per cent ethnic minority electorate).

Short-term factors

Media

The media has, in recent elections, been a very important factor in affecting voter behaviour. In the 2010 general election, 9.4 million people watched the first live TV debate, and *The Sun* newspaper was read by 8 million people every day (and for many voters this was their only source of information on the election). The media is an important factor to

> **Remember**
>
> A voter will, of course, hold more than one of these long-term factors. Age, for example, cuts across class, gender and ethnicity.

consider as it can often influence other long- and short-term factors. For instance, younger voters may be more likely to vote SNP as a result of the party's policies and image, yet this could also be because of the SNP's effective use of new media, such as Twitter, which are more often used by younger voters. It can only be assumed that as further advancements in the media continue to be made it will become an even more important factor in shaping voter attitudes

Party leadership and policies

Party leadership is a factor that has come to be a major influence on voter behaviour in recent elections.

In the 2015 UK general election, Ed Miliband, the Labour leader, was deemed to be a dull and boring leader while David Cameron was regarded as stronger and more inspiring. Arguably, this difference in leadership style had an impact on voting behaviour. However, this could also be the result of the way in which the leaders were portrayed in the popular press. In the 2017 UK general election, the campaign by the Conservative press to portray Corbyn as an incompetent radical and Prime Minister Theresa May as strong and reliable failed. May refused to take part in the leaders' debate and her campaign style lacked warmth and conviction.

Voters will not only consider *who* they are voting for, in the form of the party leaders, but they will also look at *what* they are voting for, through the party manifesto and stance on issues. Voters will be affected by the issues and policies for which a party stands. In the run-up to elections, voters will assess which policies are closest to their own values and align themselves with a party accordingly.

> ### Hints & tips ★
>
> See pages 23–26 for further information on the media.

> ### Remember 📌
>
> Although many factors affect voting behaviour, some factors are more influential than others. Social class has always been an important factor that affects voting behaviour, but more recently short-term influences seem to have overtaken social class as the most important factors.

Figure 3.4 In the 2014 Scottish referendum, 16- and 17-year-olds were allowed to vote

Chapter 4

Influencing the political process

What you should know

SQA requirements

To be successful in this section, you should know about:

★ ways in which citizens can influence government decision-making, including pressure groups.

The role and influence of pressure groups

Representative democracy does not formally permit people to make policy and influence the decision-making process directly. Instead, it allows the general public to vote for a representative, such as MPs, MSPs and councillors, who work on their behalf. However, political participation in the UK is not confined to elections, as participation continues through the activities of pressure groups. Pressure groups are groups of individuals who come together, through a common belief or passion, to put pressure on the government to introduce, abolish or change something. These groups are formed by like-minded people who feel passionate about an issue and have the aim of protecting or advancing their shared interest.

There are two main types of pressure groups: cause groups and interest groups.

Cause groups

Also sometimes known as 'promotional pressure groups', cause groups generally campaign to raise awareness of specific causes. Cause groups can campaign on behalf of other people who cannot campaign for themselves – Shelter would be an example of such a cause group – or they can attempt to influence public opinion, for example Greenpeace is an environmental group that puts pressure on the government to help create a greener world.

Interest groups

Also sometimes known as 'sectional pressure groups', interest groups work to promote a particular interest, often to advance the economic or professional status of their members, such as the British Medical Association.

To what extent do pressure groups impact on the political system?

The effectiveness of pressure groups and the extent to which they influence politics depend on the type of pressure group. Pressure groups can be either *insider* or *outsider* groups and the status of the group reflects their relationship with the government and affects the extent to which they can influence the political system.

Many pressure groups are experts in their field, such as the British Medical Association. They are known as insider pressure groups. These insider groups regularly gain direct access to policy-makers, such as civil servants or government ministers. Insider groups may even be consulted by government in the law-making process, and so they can have great power and influence on legislation. They are in a privileged position as a result of their expertise and specialist knowledge. Ultimately, insider pressure groups are able to influence government decision-making.

On the other hand, outsider groups, with no access to parliament, often mount campaigns to influence the public, government and media. They try to persuade public opinion to their point of view through activities such as demonstrations and petitions. While this type of pressure-group behaviour may earn media and public attention, it does not often result in any sort of influence on government decision-making. In fact, illegal pressure-group methods can greatly hinder the success of the pressure group in influencing the government.

However, outsider pressure groups may be successful in influencing the government, who may listen to them as a result of concerns that the group may influence large swathes of the electorate. Outsider pressure groups continually lobby government and some will use professional **lobbying** organisations, which offer contacts and knowledge of the political system. Some also try to seek pledges from candidates at elections. This strategy is used by both pro-life and pro-choice groups, for example. Other groups will take unconstitutional action, such as Fathers for Justice, who are renowned for their illegal methods of gaining media coverage.

> ## Key term
>
> **Lobbying:** When individuals or pressure groups try to influence government decisions.

Do pressure groups enhance or threaten democracy?

Remember

In the debate about the effectiveness of pressure groups, you should discuss both the strengths and the weaknesses of them.

Enhance democracy

Pressure groups greatly benefit the political system as they allow for greater participation in the political process. This is regarded as a good thing because participation in the formal political process is dwindling. In particular, election turnout is low, as is political party membership. Therefore pressure-group participation enhances democracy in the UK. The Gurkha Justice Campaign stood up for the rights of the Gurkhas who had fought for the UK during the twentieth century but who were denied the same benefits as their British and Commonwealth equivalents. After a campaign led by Joanna Lumley, the Government announced that any Gurkha who had fought in the British Army for four years or more, before 1997, would be given the right to settle in Britain.

Threaten democracy

It can also be argued that pressure groups are a threat to democracy. Unlike political parties, pressure groups are self-appointed and the public cannot vote them out in elections. This is regarded by many to be undemocratic. Pressure groups are capable of forcing minority views as they are well organised and well structured. Some pressure groups carry out illegal methods to raise their profile and gain media attention. This happened during the student protests in England and Wales in 2011, when 14 police officers were injured, statues in Parliament Square were damaged, windows were smashed and the car that was carrying Prince Charles and his wife Camilla, Duchess of Cornwall, was attacked.

The role and influence of the media in the political system

The media plays an important role in informing citizens and influencing the political process in Scotland and the UK, with the majority of the information that the public receives about politics coming from media sources. This gives the media a great deal of power, as they shape public attitude and opinion. **Free press** means that the media is not censored by the government and can openly criticise it and hold it to account. The media's influence on politics is mainly achieved through newspapers and television; however, the emergence of a sophisticated 'new media' is allowing people to stay abreast of a range of current affairs, including the world of politics.

Newspapers

Despite a decline in readership, newspapers remain the traditional medium for information, with 12 million people buying one every day. Most newspapers support a political party and are therefore biased in their reporting of stories. As newspapers are allowed to demonstrate political bias, they are very influential in politics and can persuade people to vote for political parties at election time. They can form a political alliance with a certain party and try to influence voters and shape political attitudes.

The influence of newspapers

Newspapers can be extremely influential in shaping the attitudes of the electorate. For some voters, *The Sun* is their only source of information. This makes the paper extremely powerful and important. In every election since 1992, the party backed by *The Sun* has won the election. In 2010, there was a 5 per cent swing from Labour to the Conservatives among voters; among *The Sun* readers this swing was 13.5 per cent. In addition to supporting the Conservatives in both the 2015 and 2017 general elections, *The Sun* also backed the Leave campaign. However, this was unsurprising as it has always been Eurosceptic. This paper has also been somewhat influential north of the border. In 2011 the SNP won the first majority government in Scotland and had the support of *The Sun*, so this backing may have contributed to the victory. It has also been argued that *The Sun* merely backs the party most likely to win the election, according to opinion polls.

Despite a potentially influential role in shaping public attitudes, overall newspaper readership is down. The number of newspapers bought every day is falling. Among younger people especially, papers are being replaced by newspaper apps, which send news updates, and by newspaper websites. However, the elderly who are more likely to vote are more likely to buy newspapers.

Although newspapers may continue to influence politics in the future, it will most likely be through electronic means rather than in print. Arguably the influence of newspapers on the public is declining. Nevertheless, all political parties strive to have the support of newspapers, especially with the increase over time in the number of undecided voters. In this respect, the Conservative Party has the advantage as the majority of national newspapers support the Conservatives (see Table 4.1).

Table 4.1 Political affiliation of the main UK newspapers at the 2017 general election, with their circulation as of January 2017

Newspaper	Party support	Circulation
Mail	Conservative with strong middle-class readership	1,511,357
Guardian	Labour with strong middle-class readership	156,756
Mirror	Labour with strong working-class readership	724,888
Sun	Conservative with strong working-class readership	1,666,715
Express	Conservative with UKIP leanings	392,526
Times	Conservative with strong middle-class readership	451,261
Telegraph	Conservative with strong middle-class leadership	472,258

Source: Press Gazette

Television

Unlike newspapers, television must remain politically impartial and cannot support a political party or agenda. Television channels are regulated by Ofcom, which ensures that they are not biased in their reporting. At election time, each political party is given an equal time to deliver a party political broadcast, and therefore television is an influential means through which to inform voters.

The influence of television

Live TV debates were used for the first time in the 2010 elections. The three main political parties – Labour, Conservatives and Liberal Democrats – all debated live on TV and millions tuned in to each one. Nick Clegg emerged as the 'winner' of these debates, appearing likeable and trustworthy. After the first live debate, support for the Liberal Democrats increased by 11 points – the largest ever increase during an election campaign. In two opinion polls, the Liberal Democrats overtook both Labour and the Conservatives for the first time in 100 years. However, as we know, this did not translate into actual votes at the polls. The influence of live TV debates on voting behaviour proved to be significant again in 2017 when Theresa May declined to attend the televised debate in the election that she called, instead sending Home Secretary Amber Rudd. This affected her image and the overall result as it raised issues about the quality of her leadership.

Televised leaders' debates also took place before the 2011 and 2016 Scottish Parliament Elections.

Social media

In recent years the internet has become increasingly popular, with an estimated 70 per cent of the public now accessing it on a daily basis. It provides a platform for political parties to reach out to the public and most parties now have websites, Facebook pages, Twitter feeds and YouTube channels. Political parties and politicians are making extensive use of social media to engage voters, especially young people, in politics.

The influence of new media

Newspapers and television continue to have the strongest influence on voting behaviour. In the 2010 general election, traditional media had the greatest influence on the electorate. The first TV debate was watched by 9.4 million people and *The Sun* newspaper was read by 8 million people every day. By contrast, 79 per cent of people could not recollect any online electioneering.

By the 2017 general election, the use of social media in election campaigning had become more widespread. The Conservatives made limited use of social media while the Labour Party maximised its potential in order to activate and influence young voters. In addition to the use of Facebook and Twitter, Labour realised the importance of Instagram as a platform for young people to share and promote issues. Several hashtags amassed much support for Labour: ForTheManyNotTheFew (20,063), ToriesOut (16,439) and VoteLabour (83,094) all showed strong support for Labour and were largely promoted by young people. This would suggest that young people and their prolific use of social media influenced the 2017 election.

Similarly, the SNP has made effective use of the social media advances sweeping into modern politics and, in Scotland, they are considered the trailblazers.

This does not necessarily mean that the SNP and the Labour Party are more popular. It may just be that its supporters are more likely to use social media. However, it does ensure that they have a very effective means through which to inform and persuade voters. Social media appears to be a potential path to power that was previously unimaginable.

It is widely acknowledged that as new media continues to develop, its influence on politics will become greater. Social media is allowing citizens to become journalists and to participate and interact more than traditional forms of the media allow. Overall, newspapers and television are changing the ways they engage with their readers and viewers. Arguably, this better reflects demands from the electorate, especially the young, and how they access information.

Hints & tips

In an analysis/evaluation question on the effectiveness of Parliament in holding the government to account, you should include the role of House of Lords if you have studies the UK Government.

Table 4.2 Number of Twitter followers (taken from Scottish political party Twitter pages)

Party	Number of Twitter followers	
	July 2014	April 2018
SNP	34,600	207,120
Labour	11,100	35,844
Greens	8,967	46,306
Conservatives	4,592	23,310
Liberal Democrats	3,672	11,364

Key points !

The Leveson Inquiry as an example of the control of the media

In 2012, the Leveson Inquiry was held into the freedom of the press. The inquiry was set up as a result of allegations of phone hacking from celebrities and members of the public by the now defunct *News of the World*. As a result of the Leveson Inquiry, a Royal Charter was announced to protect the freedom of the press while also protecting the public from the abuses committed by the media prior to the inquiry.

Figure 4.1 Live TV debates were used for the first time in the 2010 elections

Chapter 5

Representative democracy in Scotland and the UK

What you should know

SQA requirements

To be successful in this section, you should know about:

★ the effectiveness of parliamentary representatives in holding government to account.

Remember

You will have studied in depth the effectiveness of representatives in either the UK Parliament or the Scottish Parliament. In the UK Parliament you may consider both the House of Commons and House of Lords. In the Scottish Parliament there is no second chamber and it is select committees that hold the Scottish Government to account.

The role of political representatives

The UK is a representative democracy, which means that the electorate votes in elections for the people they want to represent them. These representatives then make decisions on behalf of the electorate. MPs and MSPs have both mandatory and discretionary roles and responsibilities that they carry out.

Key term

Scrutinise: To examine something closely.

Table 5.1 The role of an MP

MPs	
Vote in the House of Commons	One of the most important roles of an MP is the power to vote in the House of Commons. Before a bill can be passed as legislation, MPs must individually vote 'Aye' or 'No'. MPs will usually vote in line with their party's wishes but their voting decision should be made on behalf of their constituency. In June 2015, the European Referendum Bill was passed in the Commons by 544 votes to 53, which allowed the EU referendum to take place on 23 June 2016.
Attend adjournment debates	Debates are held in the chamber on a daily basis, providing MPs with the opportunity to represent their constituents in Parliament. In debates, the executive is forced to account for its actions. Adjournment debates allow backbench MPs to speak on an issue of importance to their constituents.
Attend Question Time	MPs are given the opportunity to question a government minister on an issue in the House of Commons. This gives MPs the opportunity to **scrutinise** the work of the government. Most of the questions are 'seen' questions, where ministers are allowed to prepare an answer beforehand. The questions are chosen by the Speaker of the House and, as the vast majority are not able to be asked in the allocated time, written answers are given to these instead.
Attend Prime Minister's Questions (PMQs)	PMQs takes place every Wednesday and during this time the prime minister is questioned by MPs about government decisions and current affairs. Although this may not necessarily affect government decision-making, it does affect party popularity and how a leader is viewed. ⇨

MPs	
Membership of committees	Most MPs are members of committees in the House of Commons. Committees give MPs an opportunity to scrutinise the work of the government and influence a specific area of decision-making. Committees reflect the balance of power held in the House of Commons and therefore if a party holds a large majority, it can be difficult for the committees to challenge the government effectively. There are different committees in Parliament, including Select, Public bills and backbench business committees.
Propose Private Members' Bills	MPs also have the opportunity to propose their own bills. At the beginning of each parliamentary session, 20 applications for Private Members' Bills are selected to be debated for a whole day by the House of Commons. Private Members' Bills rarely reach the later stages of the legislative process (see Table 5.2).
Undertake constituency work	MPs have important roles and duties that must be carried out in their constituency. The most important role in the constituency is to hold regular surgeries. However, they must also attend meetings in the local community, visit local areas and attend social events and maintain a high profile in the local media.

Table 5.2 Success rate of public bills which start the legislative process in the House of Commons

Session	Percentage of Government Bills receiving royal assent	Percentage of Private Members' Bills receiving royal assent
2007–2008	92	3
2010–2012	89	3
2014–2015	100	6

Source: *Politics Review*, November 2016

Remember

Reforms have been made to strengthen the effectiveness of UK committees. Chairpersons are now elected by secret ballots, and other members are also chosen by their parties via secret ballots, thus reducing the whips' influence. A backbench business committee determines business before the House on 35 days per session.

Table 5.3 The role of an MSP

MSPs	
Propose motions and debates	MSPs are able to propose motions in Parliament. These motions can be about local, national or international issues that affect Scotland.
Attend Question Time	Similar to the system in Westminster, every Thursday morning MSPs participate in a general Question Time whereby government ministers are questioned on their departments. Written questions can also be submitted. Every Thursday afternoon, First Minister's Question Time is held, where the first minister is questioned on issues.
Join committees	Committees exist to scrutinise the work of the Scottish Government and may conduct inquiries into specific areas. In 2012 the Economy, Energy and Tourism Committee conducted an inquiry into the Government's green energy target. Donald Trump was called as a witness as he is regarded as an expert on tourism. He gave evidence on the effect of wind farms on tourism. From 2011 until 2016, the SNP had a majority in each of the committees, which weakened the ability of opposition parties to scrutinise SNP policy. Committees also have the power to propose new bills.
Vote at Decision Time	A further role of MSPs is to vote on issues in Parliament. At the end of parliamentary days, MSPs can vote at Decision Time, where votes are passed on any issues debated that day. MSPs are normally instructed how to vote by their political party.

Pressures on representatives

The main role for both MPs and MSPs is to represent constituents. However, as they also remain answerable to their political party, they can find themselves with conflicting pressures. Representatives must try to satisfy their constituents, their party, **whips**, pressure groups and the media, while also upholding their personal beliefs and values. This can result in a range of conflicting loyalties.

Constituency

First and foremost, an MP should represent the constituents who elected them. Obviously it is vital for MPs to placate their constituents given that they may well not be re-elected at the next election.

The political party

Most MPs are elected not for their own personal qualities but because it is believed that they will put into action the policies of their political party. Therefore the MP represents both their constituents and their political party. The MP must remain loyal to their party as they will know that they may only have been elected as a result of their membership to that party.

The Party Whip system

To ensure that MPs carry out the wishes of the party, whips are employed to put pressure on the MP to support the party. If an MP votes against the party's wishes, they may be expelled and it will be unlikely that they will be able to gain the necessary public support to be re-elected at the next election.

Key term

Whips: Officials of a political party appointed to maintain parliamentary discipline among its members.

The role of the legislature

Parliament has two houses: the House of Commons and the House of Lords. The Commons is the more important of the two as the Lords are unelected and their powers are limited.

The House of Commons

The House of Commons consists of 650 MPs, each representing a single constituency. MPs consider and propose new laws and can scrutinise government policies by asking ministers questions about current issues, either in the Commons Chamber or in committees.

Hints & tips

In an evaluation question on the effectiveness of parliament in holding the UK government to account, you should include reference to the House of Lords.

Table 5.4 The work of the House of Commons

House of Commons	
Legislation	All MPs are involved in amending bills and passing laws. One of the main functions of the House of Commons is to legislate. The government will enjoy more power in the House if it has returned a working majority. Thanks to the First Past The Post electoral system, the House is normally controlled by the governing party, which limits the extent to which the government is actually scrutinised by the House of Commons. In August 2013, backbench MPs revolted against their government when 40 coalition MPs went against their chief whip by voting against military action in Syria. MPs are clearly able to influence legislation through their role in the House of Commons.
Committees	Selected MPs sit on committees that are responsible for scrutinising proposed legislation and the work of government departments.
Scrutiny	All MPs are responsible for scrutinising the work of the government through questioning at Question Time and participating in debates.

The House of Lords

The House of Lords is the unelected branch of Parliament and therefore does not directly represent the people of the UK. Those who are members of the Lords are usually referred to as peers. Although the House of Lords usually gives way to the will of the House of Commons, this branch of the legislature does also carry out a number of roles.

Table 5.5 The work of the House of Lords

House of Lords	
Debate	Peers in the House of Lords have party affiliations but they tend to be less partisan than MPs in the Commons. Furthermore, they have the opportunity to debate issues in a less politically biased way than the more confrontational House of Commons. It has been argued that legislation is therefore improved by their contributions. No party has a majority in the House of Lords, and as such governments must win cross-party support for their legislation.
Legislation	Most bills are passed by the House of Lords before becoming law. However, if the House of Lords rejects a non-financial bill that has been passed by the House of Commons in two consecutive parliamentary sessions, it automatically becomes law.
Scrutiny	The House of Lords plays an active role in scrutinising the work of the government. The 2010–2015 coalition government experienced 99 defeats in the Lords, especially on welfare reforms. In session 2014–2015, almost one in three of the 3,450 amendments made by the Lords were accepted.

Remember

The impact and limitations of both coalition and minority governments

The House of Lords Reform Bill 2012, which proposed a mainly elected House of Lords, was introduced by Nick Clegg. It became clear that the Government was going to lose the vote on the 'programme motion' and it was later withdrawn. At the vote on whether to give the bill a second reading, 91 Conservative MPs voted against the three-line whip, while 19 more abstained. Deputy Prime Minister Nick Clegg announced that the Government was abandoning the bill due to the opposition from Conservative backbench MPs, claiming that the Conservatives had 'broken the coalition contract'. In this instance, the existence of a coalition government limited the law-making process in Westminster. As a result, the Liberal Democrats pledged to vote against proposed constituency boundary changes designed to reduce the size of the Commons from 650 to 600 MPs.

This shows how coalition governments can be a barrier to effective law-making in the UK Government when consensus cannot be reached.

Likewise, minority governments can limit the law-making process. In May 2017, while the Conservatives won the most votes and seats, they lost their majority in the House of Commons. Theresa May formed a minority government with 317 seats. Subsequently a confidence and supply arrangement with the Democratic Unionist Party (DUP) was made. The DUP agreed to support the Government on all motions of confidence, and on the Queen's Speech, the Budget, finance bills, money bills, supply and appropriation legislation and Estimates. In return for the confidence and supply agreement, the Conservative Party agreed there would be £1 billion extra public spending in Northern Ireland.

The scrutiny powers of representatives tend to be greater if there is a coalition and minority governments. With the absence of an overall majority, such governments must compromise and negotiate more with backbench MPs from all parties to ensure that they do not lose the vote in Parliament. However the DUP regarded Mrs May's Brexit agreement with the EU as a betrayal of the unity of the UK (Northern Ireland would have different arrangements from the rest of the UK). As a result, they did not support the Government by opposing an opposition motion to deem the Government in being in contempt of Parliament. On the 5th December, the Government lost three humiliating votes with the opposition parties declaring that "Parliament had won back control of Brexit".

The role of the UK and Scottish Executive

The Executive is comprised of the prime minister, the Cabinet and the Civil Service. Unlike the USA, the UK does not have a 'written' constitution that details the powers of elected representatives. This means that the role of the Executive cannot be found in one single document; instead, the British Constitution is embodied in several documents.

Table 5.6 The role of the prime minister

Prime minister	
Leader of the governing party	First and foremost, the PM is the leader of the governing party. They are the person that the public associates with that party. As the leader of the party, it is the PM's responsibility to manage their MPs, and this is achieved through the use of the whip system. Whips have an important role to play, especially in governments with a small majority. It is the whips' job to ensure that every member turns out to vote on the majority votes taking place in Parliament. 'Three-line whips' are imposed on significant occasions, such as motions of no confidence.
Appoint Cabinet ministers	The PM is responsible for appointing members to the Cabinet. This is known as the power of **patronage**. Furthermore, the PM is able to reshuffle Cabinet ministers whenever they wish. Most MPs are ambitious and would like to be appointed to the Cabinet and therefore they tend to remain loyal to the party and to their leader. Not only will the PM appoint their allies to the Cabinet, but they may also leave outside the Cabinet those whom they deem to be too powerful.
Appoint peers	The UK honours system allows individuals to be recognised for various achievements and services to their country. Many value the honour of a seat in the House of Lords. The PM has responsibility for appointing many of these honours.

> **Key term**
>
> **Patronage:** The power to control appointments to particular positions.

Table 5.7 The role of the first minister

First minister	
Leader of the governing party	Like the PM, the first minister is simply the leader of the governing party. When the SNP returned a majority to the Scottish Parliament in 2011, Alex Salmond enjoyed a particularly powerful position regarding the introduction of new laws. As a result, the bills that passed through normally became law, as was the case with the Scottish Independence Referendum Bill (2013). Currently Nicola Sturgeon leads a minority government and therefore needs the support of other parties to pass legislation.
Powers of patronage	Like the PM, the first minister has powers of patronage – to appoint who they want to the Cabinet. MSPs are appointed by the first minister from their party to run government departments. The first minister must also chair the Cabinet meetings on Wednesday mornings, and they have the power to reshuffle the Cabinet.

The role of the Cabinet

The Cabinet is the ultimate decision-making body of the executive. It is made up of the heads of key departments, legal officers and government whips and headed by the prime minister. The prime minister is supposed to be *primus inter pares* – the first among equals – but some critics have suggested that a more presidential approach has been adopted by recent prime ministers. Cabinet ministers must support all Cabinet decisions and government policy. This is known as **collective responsibility**. Cabinet ministers are held accountable for their department.

Similarly, the Scottish Cabinet comprises MSPs selected by the first minister to run certain departments. The Scottish Cabinet normally meets weekly at Bute House in Edinburgh, and also operates on the basis of collective responsibility.

The role of the Civil Service

Within the Executive branch there is a non-political or a neutral element known as the Civil Service. While government ministers make the policy, civil servants administer those decisions. Unlike politicians who are elected to their positions, civil servants are permanent appointees who are not responsible for the success or failure of departments. As civil servants can remain in departments for many years, unlike elected ministers, they can acquire expert knowledge in certain areas. The Civil Service is a matter reserved to UK Parliament and therefore the Civil Service in Scotland remains part of the Home Civil Service. However, Scottish civil servants are accountable to Scottish ministers, who are themselves accountable to the Scottish Parliament.

Opportunities to scrutinise the respective Executives

UK Parliament

- Votes in the House of Commons can give backbench MPs the opportunity to rebel. In October 2013, a total of 81 of David Cameron's MPs voted for a Commons motion calling for a referendum on Britain's relationship with the EU, even though the Prime Minister had ordered his party to oppose it. This resulted in the EU referendum in 2016 in which the electorate voted to leave the EU.
- Prime Minister's Question Time gives MPs from both the governing and the opposition parties the ability to question the prime minister. Prime Minister's Question Time may not necessarily affect policy but it does change the way that a party is viewed by the electorate.
- Select Committees scrutinise the work of the government. Membership of committees reflects party strength and so they are dominated by the governing party, which can limit the ability of the opposition party to hold the Executive to account.

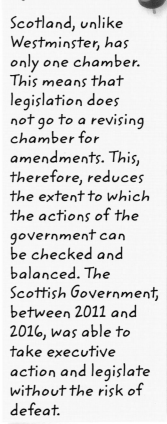

Remember

Scotland, unlike Westminster, has only one chamber. This means that legislation does not go to a revising chamber for amendments. This, therefore, reduces the extent to which the actions of the government can be checked and balanced. The Scottish Government, between 2011 and 2016, was able to take executive action and legislate without the risk of defeat.

- Opposition Days are set aside as an opportunity for opposition parties to criticise government policy. Opposition parties generally use these as opportunities to try to embarrass the Executive.
- The House of Lords effectively challenges the Executive and limits its power. As lords are unelected, this challenge is more effective because they are more independent than MPs. Furthermore, most have already enjoyed a political career and so are not influenced by the prospect of career advancements from the prime minister.

Scottish Parliament

- Much like in Westminster, voting in the Scottish Parliament allows the legislative to limit the power of the Executive. However, as a result of the SNP majority government elected in 2011, the extent to which opposition parties could prevent the government from being too powerful was limited. In 2012 the Scotland Act was passed, which allowed the Scottish Government to hold the 2014 referendum on Scottish independence.
- Similarly, while committees offer opportunities to ensure a balance of power, they have been dominated by the SNP since 2011 and have therefore had a limited ability to hold the Executive to account (see below).
- First Minister's Question Time gives MSPs from the governing and opposition parties the chance to question the government on its actions. This can have an effect on the way in which the first minister and their party are viewed.

These methods all ensure that both the UK and Scottish Executives do not hold too much power and that there remains a balance of power between the legislature and the Executive.

Conflict of interest in Select Committees

In 2016, Labour MSP Neil Findlay was refused permission at a Justice committee session to ask questions of the then Police Scotland chief, Phil Gormley, about his controversial role in the discredited and now disbanded Special Demonstration Squad by the committee's SNP convenor. In the press, he stated, 'Before entering the [Scottish] Parliament five years ago, I was told the committee system was the "jewel in the crown" of the Parliament … the reality is that the committees are controlled by government majorities. Too many MSPs [SNP] sitting on them never utter a word of criticism against their own government and simply fall into line and do ministers' bidding.'

Opposition parties have condemned the recent practice of SNP committee members acting as assistants (parliamentary liaison officers or PLOs) to ministers. This, it is argued, is a conflict of interest as these PLOs act as the 'eyes and ears' of the minister. Their role in the Select Committees is to effectively scrutinise and if necessary criticise ministers and issue reports, which may be critical. It should be noted that the Westminster equivalent of PLOs are banned from being involved in any business associated with the minister they work for.

Part Three: Social issues in the UK

This section of the book provides summary course notes for the Social Issues in the UK area of study.

You will have studied one of the following topics as part of your Higher Social Issues area of study:
- Social Inequality
- Crime and the Law.

In the extended response/essay section of the exam, you will answer either a 12-mark question or a 20-mark question.

Chapter 6
Social inequality

Evidence of social inequality

Poverty

The UK and Scottish Governments define poverty by relating it to a household's income. You are considered to be living in **relative poverty** if your income is less than 60 per cent of the UK average income. This 'poverty line' stood at £350 per week in 2018 for a household with two adults and two children under 13.

Classifications and causes of poverty

- **Persistent poverty:** Where someone experiences long periods of poverty, possibly due to long-term unemployment. Once trapped in poverty, families can spend generations within the poverty trap. Some 3.7 million working-age households have no one in employment (18 per cent of total households).
- **Recurrent poverty:** Many occupations are cyclical in nature. Those working in outdoor activities such as skiing may find that during the summer months they experience poverty.
- **The impact of the world banking crisis of 2008 and government spending cuts:** According to the Joseph Rowntree Foundation, the average incomes of the lowest social groups, known as DE, have fallen by 10 per cent since 2008.
- **The gap between the costs of essentials and real wages is widening:** According to a Joseph Rowntree Foundation report in July 2018, the rising costs of transport, childcare and energy has left low-income families needing one-third more money to make ends meet compared to ten years ago. Travel is 65 per cent more expensive, the average cost of food is 25 per cent more expensive and energy bills are 40 per cent more expensive.

Key terms

Absolute poverty:
A measure of whether the income of the poorest households is keeping pace with inflation.

Relative poverty:
Households whose income is less than 60 per cent of average incomes in the UK. In 2018, a couple with two children are living in relative poverty if they are living on less than £350 a week.

Causes and impact of social inequality

A June 2014 report by the Poverty Action Group stated that people were being blamed for being poor and it was assumed that they were work shy. The reality is that more than half of Scots suffering poverty and social exclusion live in working households trapped in low-paid jobs and zero-hours contracts. This contradicts the UK Government's view that 'work is the best route out of poverty'.

According to the Joseph Rowntree Foundation (JRF), a single person needed to earn at least £18,400 a year in 2018 to reach a 'minimum income standard' and afford a socially acceptable standard of living.

Campbell Robb, the Chief Executive of JRF stated 'Some working parents are actually further away from reaching a decent living standard because tax credits to top up low wages have been falling when families need them most' (Joseph Rowntree Foundation).

Third sector (voluntary) groups work hard to highlight wealth and poverty inequality and to assess the impact of government policies (see page 57). Third sector groups such as the Joseph Rowntree Foundation, Oxfam and End Child Poverty Coalition provide evidence on the extent of social inequality as outlined below.

JRF Poverty Report, December 2017

The main findings of the report were:

- Child and pensioner poverty is rising and places the progress made over the last two decades towards reducing poverty in peril.
- 14 million people in the UK currently live in poverty – more than one in five of the population.
- Since the introduction of the welfare reforms, a further 700,000 UK children and pensioners have fallen into relative poverty (300,000 pensioners and 400,000 children).
- The increase in child poverty can be linked to a freeze on benefits, a reduction in tax credits and stagnant wages for low-income families. (Data released by HM Revenue and Customs in July 2018 highlights that the income of people earning more than £150,000 has increased by 89 per cent since the Conservatives came to power in 2010. In contrast, those earning less than £20,000 have seen their incomes increase by only 1.8 per cent over the same period.)

Source: Joseph Rowntree Foundation

Reasons why income/wealth inequalities exist

Social exclusion

Living on low income leads to **social exclusion**, limiting the lifestyle opportunities for individuals and families. They may have feelings of hopelessness, experience low self-esteem and have a low expectation of living a meaningful life. This 'poverty trap' creates a cycle of poverty that is repeated by the next generation.

> **Key term**
>
> **Social exclusion:** The impact of poverty on individuals and groups and the extent to which they are unable to participate in aspects of society, for example education, health and housing, due to being in poverty.

Groups at risk of social exclusion

- Those with low levels of skills due to poor education.
- Unemployment or low-paid work may result in some people not being able to participate in social networks, such as membership of exercise clubs or activity groups.
- Children from lower income backgrounds may not be able to participate in many activities, such as school trips or after-school clubs. This can affect their self-esteem and contribute towards the cycle of poverty.
- Disability and long-term ill-health are also more likely to result in social exclusion as there is less access to employment and increased living costs.
- Elderly people who depend totally on the state pension can struggle to cover rising living costs and may experience fuel poverty.
- Women are generally at a higher risk of poverty as they are more likely to be involved in unpaid care, to be in lower paid employment or part-time work and tend to have lower pensions.
- Ethnic minority groups may experience social exclusion due to discrimination, racism and poor housing.

Benefits system and low pay

The 2017 JRF Report blames the significant government cuts to welfare payments as being one of the factors in widening wealth inequality. The Conservative Government's emphasis on individual responsibility, reflected in the roll out of the controversial Universal Credit, is also listed as being to blame.

However, the UK Government disagrees and argues that welfare reforms are helping the poor. A Department for Work and Pensions spokesperson stated: 'The truth is that employment is up and unemployment is falling and our vital reforms are working. We are returning fairness to the welfare system and helping people lift themselves out of poverty by making work pay. We are transforming the lives of the poorest people in society … keeping the benefits bill sustainable, so we can support people when they need it most.'

Unemployment has fallen significantly from 8.2 per cent in 2012 to 4.2 per cent in 2018, but poverty rates have not declined. This is because there has been a massive increase in employers using low-paid **zero-hour contracts**. The unemployed may have their benefits stopped if they refuse to accept a zero-hour contract. As a result, there has been a significant increase in the number of working poor, especially those with families. The massive increase in the use of food banks would support criticism of the government (see page 39).

> ## Key term
>
> **Zero-hour contract:** A contract in which the employee does not have a fixed number of hours in their working week. They will only be paid for the hours they work, which will vary from week to week. Employers do not need to pay pension contributions or redundancy pay.

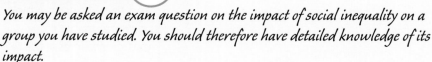

Hints & tips

You may be asked an exam question on the impact of social inequality on a group you have studied. You should therefore have detailed knowledge of its impact.

Food banks

In 2017 the Trussell Trust, the UK's biggest food bank network whose annual figures provide a broad measure of social inequality, gave out a record 1.3 million food parcels, up 13 per cent from the previous year. Food banks in areas where the full Universal Credit service had been in place for 12 months or more were four times as busy, recording an average increase in three-day emergency packages (see also page 57).

Oxfam Scotland stated: 'Food banks provide invaluable support for families on the breadline, but the fact they are needed in Scotland in the twenty-first century is a stain on our national conscience. Too many people need more help to deal with the consequences of stagnating wages, insecure work and rising food and fuel prices'.

Figure 6.1 A food bank in Scotland

Causes and impact of social inequality on selected groups

Elderly people

In 2018, it was estimated that 1.9 million elderly people were living below the official poverty line. Of that figure, 1 million lived in severe poverty (defined as below 50 per cent of the average income after housing costs).

Pensioners who do not have a works pension and whose only income is their state pension struggle financially. Almost one in four of single pensioner households who depend solely on their state pension experience poverty.

In the UK, about one-third of all pensioner households entitled to pension credit are not claiming it – this equates to 1.3 million households. For this reason, pressure groups are against **means-tested benefits** for elderly people.

Table 6.1 The cost of benefits for elderly people

Cost	Benefit
£2 billion	Winter Fuel Payment of £200 per household/ £300 for over-80s
£1 billion	Free bus passes in England and Wales
£600 million	Free television licences for over-75s

Key terms

Means-tested benefits: A person must be on a low or designated income to be entitled to the benefit, for example child benefit.

Universal benefits: Individuals receive the benefits regardless of their income, for example state pensions and free prescriptions (excluding England).

Views of organisations

'We strongly oppose any move to more means-testing of older people. It leaves out many people who need money but do not claim, and it is complex, inefficient and costly in terms of administration. Worse still, it penalises those who have saved, whereas **universal benefits** are straightforward and ensure all those who need them receive what they should.'

Saga (pressure group for elderly people)

'It is very noticeable that wealthy pensioners are the one group that have not been affected by the austerity programme as a whole.'

Institute of Fiscal Studies

Fuel poverty

The official definition of 'fuel poverty' is when a household must pay more than 10 per cent of its disposable income to heat their home to an adequate level. Since 2010 it is estimated that energy prices have increased by 37 per cent, and this has led to dramatic increases in fuel poverty. The elderly especially suffer from fuel poverty as they spend so much of their time in their home.

Child poverty

Poverty has a devastating effect on children growing up. It affects their whole life, from health and wellbeing to educational attainment and aspirations (see Social inequality and health, pages 42–47).

There were 3.5 million children living in poverty in the UK in 2017: 27 per cent of children, or more than one in four. At a local level, statistics are even more concerning in some areas. In the Calton area of Glasgow, 49 per cent of children live in poverty. In Glasgow, Manchester and Liverpool, approximately one-third of all children live below the poverty line.

Child poverty in the UK: Facts and figures

- In 2015, 3.5 million children (27 per cent) were living in poverty in the UK. This was the lowest level for this figure since the 1990s when it peaked at 34 per cent. However, the figure is now rising (see page 37).
- Babies from disadvantaged families are more likely to be born underweight – an average of 200 grams lower than babies from the richest families.
- Children from low-income households are nearly three times more likely to suffer mental health problems than children from more affluent households.
- Children living in poverty are almost twice as likely to live in bad housing. This has significant effects on both their physical and mental health, as well as their educational achievement.
- Children who are from socially deprived backgrounds are more likely to be obese due to a poor diet of junk food and cheap ready meals.
- Figures published in 2018 highlight that the number of overweight children is slightly falling. However, this is because the rates are declining in the more affluent areas but they are still increasing in the poorest areas. Table 6.2 applies to England but the same trend is taking place in Scotland.

Table 6.2 Ten- and eleven-year-olds who are overweight in England, as a percentage of the total

	2006	2010	2012	2014	2016
Poorest decile	35	37	37	38	39
Average	33	34	34	35	34
Richest decile	26	27	26	26	25

Source: Public Health England, 2018

Social inequality and education

Children growing up in poorer families leave school with substantially lower levels of educational attainment. This begins in primary 1, where pupils from a deprived background can be up to a year behind their middle-class counterparts developmentally, and lack basic skills such as problem-solving and literacy.

Nicola Sturgeon, Scotland's first minister, has made it a priority of the Government to close the attainment gap between schools in deprived areas and those in affluent areas and to increase the number of students from the poorest areas attending Scottish universities.

Policies to close the attainment gap

With education a devolved matter, the SNP has followed a different path from England. Scottish students do not pay university fees, which are more than £9000 a year in England.

Education Maintenance Allowance (EMA)

This is a grant given to students from low-income families who attend school or college to encourage these students to continue their education. It is hoped that this will improve their future employment opportunities. (The EMA has been scrapped in England.)

Scottish Pupil Equity Fund

In both 2017 and 2018 the Scottish Government allocated £120 million to 2300 schools to improve attainment. The amount a school receives is based on the level of deprivation which is calculated according to free school meals entitlement.

University uptake

The Scottish Government has set targets for universities to achieve a 20 per cent uptake of places by 2030 from the poorest 20 per cent of the student cohort. New universities, such as Abertay, take 15 per cent of their students from the 20 per cent of the most deprived areas. However, the ancient universities have a much lower intake of these students, with only 8 per cent of the students at Edinburgh University coming from this group. The ancient universities are being encouraged to practise positive discrimination by allowing students from this group to enter university with lower qualifications.

The Scottish Government points to the fact that more Scottish students, including those from the poorest areas, are going to university – the 2018 figures show that more than 40 per cent of school-leavers went on to higher education, which is a record number. More importantly, the attainment gap among the social classes is narrowing: 41.5 per cent of the poorest income students achieve at least one Higher compared to only 24 per cent in 2009. However, less than a quarter of the poorest income students go to university, compared to 61 per cent from the most affluent areas.

Positive discrimination

Students who apply to Glasgow University from areas of multiple deprivation can be provided with reduced exam requirements for entry to their course. This is to compensate for the disadvantages that they face growing up. Critics have argued that the universities are 'dumbing down' academic integrity. Research indicates, however, that these students do just as well as those accepted with higher grades.

Figure 6.2 Students at Glasgow University

Unemployed young adults

The unemployment rate for 16- to 24-year-olds is now more than four times the rate of older workers. The unemployment rate among 16- and 17-year-olds is 36 per cent, and 18 per cent among 18- to 24-year-olds. This compares to 4.7 per cent among 35- to 49-year-olds. Unemployment of young people, especially in cities, can lead to a host of major societal issues, for example poverty, social exclusion, drug abuse and crime, and their related impacts on the individual's physical and mental wellbeing. Tony Blair, a former prime minister, stated: 'a big cause of the riots in England in 2011 was an alienated, disaffected youth … outside the social mainstream'.

Social inequality and health

Despite the achievements of the NHS, there is clear evidence that a person's social position, gender, ethnic origin and the area in which they live can affect their chances of achieving good health. One school of thought argues that poverty is the most crucial factor related to health and cites numerous reports to support this viewpoint. Their solution is a collectivist approach to tackling the social and economic impact of social exclusion. In contrast, the individualist approach states that all citizens have access to the NHS and must take responsibility for their own health; that obesity, smoking and the over-consumption of alcohol are lifestyle choices.

Individualist and collectivist debate

This debate centres on the role of the state in meeting the needs of society. All political parties would argue that the existence of the Welfare State including the National Health Service displays the collectivist approach of the nation. It is the duty of the state to look after the health of all its citizens, to financially support those who cannot work and to provide for the elderly and the disabled. The NHS is a treasured institution and regarded as the symbol of collectivism – providing a service 'from the cradle to the grave'.

Individualists would argue that people who are obese, smoke or drink too much are to blame for their poor health, and that the state should only provide minimum support for those who are able-bodied and unemployed. They would argue that the Welfare State has created a dependency culture where some individuals are too lazy to work or decide that they will get more from state benefits than from employment. They would also argue that individual choice is being reduced by the 'nanny state'.

The Conservative Party has, traditionally, been more sympathetic to the individualist viewpoint. Since 2010, Conservative governments have justified their reforms of social security benefits as an attempt to encourage individuals to display greater self-reliance and for the able-bodied unemployed to return to work (see more on welfare reforms, pages 50–52).

Collectivists would argue that inequalities between the social classes are to blame for poor life choices. Living on a low income, in sub-standard housing on a run-down estate can lead to low self-esteem and feelings of hopelessness and depression. They argue that the solution to poor health is to adopt a collectivist approach and reduce the social inequalities which lead to health inequalities.

Figure 6.3 People who live in deprived areas experience poor health

Geographic inequalities

There is a clear north–south divide in the health of the British public. Life expectancy for men is lower in Scotland than in England: 77.1 compared to 79.2.

There are areas in Scotland and northern England, however, that compare favourably with the healthiest areas in the south-east of England, while parts of London have poor health comparable with the most deprived areas in the country. It is clear that social class and lifestyle play a crucial role.

Evidence of the link between poverty and poor health

The Black Report 1980

Numerous reports have highlighted the link between poverty and poor health. The first and therefore the most famous was the Black Report in 1980. This enquiry into inequalities in health established for the first time a clear link between socio-economic groups and health.

The Acheson Report 1998

This report provided a comprehensive survey of the condition of disadvantaged people, and its conclusion echoed the Black Report – that poverty had to be tackled through concerted government action and a policy of social inclusion in education, housing, employment, social services and health provision.

The CACI Report 2006

The CACI Report highlighted the north–south health divide and confirmed the shockingly unhealthy lifestyles of a significant number of Scots (Scottish regions account for 22 out of the top 25 UK illness areas). The report found that Scots are more likely to suffer long-term illness, take less exercise, be more overweight and spend more on cigarettes and alcohol than other Britons.

The WHO Report 2008

The World Health Organization Report concluded that 'social injustice is killing people on a grand scale; for instance a boy in the Calton district of Glasgow's East End is likely to live to 54, but just a few miles away in the prosperous suburb of Lenzie, average male life expectancy rises to 82.

National Records of Scotland Report 2017

While life expectancy has steadily improved for all social groups there is still a significant gap between those living in the 20 per cent most deprived areas and those living in the 20 per cent most affluent areas – for males, the gap is 10.5 years and for females, 7.8 years.

PopChange data resource 2018 report

The report 'PopChange: Population Change and Geographic Inequalities in Britain, 1971–2011: Deprivation Change in Britain' by academics from Liverpool University used census data from the last 40 years to pinpoint areas of deprivation by examining 120,000 neighbourhoods. Unsurprisingly, the areas that have experienced a large increase in deprivation are in the urban parts of the country. Glasgow has the ten most deprived areas in Britain, with the Calton area having three of the most deprived areas. These are the areas which suffer most from health inequalities.

The biology of poverty

Harry Burns, the former chief medical officer for Scotland, referred to the west of Scotland as experiencing a 'biology of poverty'. The collapse of heavy industry, generations of male unemployment and a breakdown in family and community relationships has affected generations of children and created a cycle of entrapment.

Three Cities Report 2010

This research examined the health and death rates of the citizens of Glasgow, Manchester and Liverpool between 2003 and 2007 – cities with broadly similar deprivation figures. Yet:

- there are 900 extra deaths per year in Glasgow compared to Manchester and Liverpool
- Glasgow's cancer and heart disease deaths are well above those of Manchester and Liverpool
- more disturbing are the alcohol- and drugs-related deaths in Glasgow – more than double the figures of the other two cities.

Lifestyle issues

Individualists argue that although social inequality can be a factor, it is bad lifestyle choices that create poor health, as indicated in Figure 6.4. However, this view is challenged by those who argue that social inequality has a detrimental impact on lifestyle choices and quality of life: living in a damp home surrounded by a drab and depressing environment, with limited life opportunities and choices, has a negative effect on health.

> **Remember**
>
> A popular exam question is the main causes of health inequalities in Scotland/UK. A key issue centres over the individualist/collective debate. Is it simply poor lifestyle choices, or is poverty the key cause?

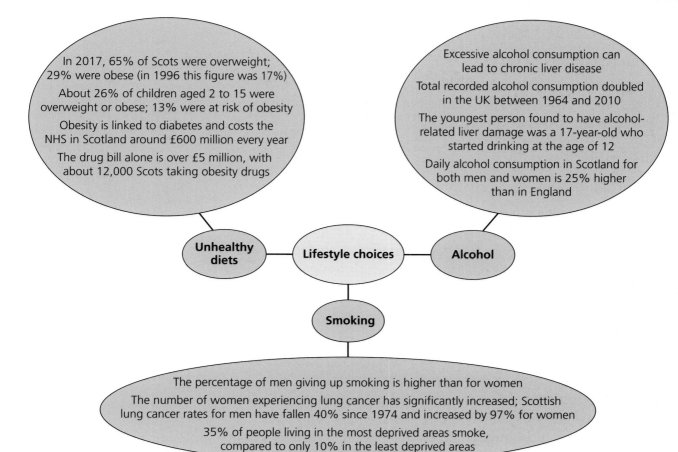

Figure 6.4 Lifestyle choices

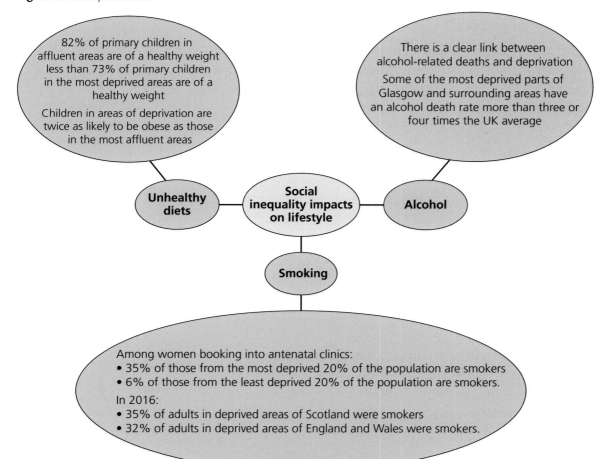

Figure 6.5 Social inequality impacts on lifestyle

Government responses to health inequalities

Health is a devolved issue and both the Labour/Liberal Democrats and SNP Governments have tried to improve the health of the Scottish people and to reduce health inequalities.

Key initiatives

Increased UK and Scottish spending on health

In England, health spending rose from £34 billion in 1998 to £90 billion in 2008–2009; and in Scotland from £4.6 million to £10.3 million in the same period. Since 2010, the austerity cuts have been less severe for the NHS than for other services, such as education. The health service is struggling, however, to cope with an ageing population and the rise of obesity and its associated illnesses.

Free prescriptions and eye tests in Scotland

In 2011, Scotland followed the example of Wales and introduced free prescriptions. Nicola Sturgeon, then deputy first minister, stated: 'Prescription charges are a tax on ill health, and can be a barrier to good health for too many people. This Scottish Government is committed to building a healthier nation; through tackling the health inequalities that still scar our nation and supporting people to live longer and lead healthier lives.'

Measures to reduce smoking

In 2006 in Scotland and in 2007 in England, smoking was banned in public places. Other actions put in place banned tobacco sales from vending machines and raised the legal age for buying tobacco from 16 to 18. In 2017, it became illegal to smoke in a car with someone under the age of 18 present.

Measures to tackle obesity

UK and Scottish government health campaigns have raised awareness. The *Sunday Herald*, with the support of the medical profession, launched a campaign to persuade retailers not to sell high-energy drinks such as Red Bull to children under 16. *Hungry for Success* campaigns in schools have been introduced to promote healthy eating.

All primary 1–3 pupils receive a free school meal that promotes healthy living.

Sugar tax

In 2018, a UK sugar tax was introduced on soft drinks with a sugar content above 5g per 100ml. Drinks such as Irn-Bru, Pepsi and Coke in their original form will have the tax imposed. It is estimated that the tax will raise £520 million a year, which will be spent on promoting healthy lifestyles.

Tackling alcohol abuse

In May 2018, the Scottish Government finally introduced Minimum Unit Pricing (MUP), which was set at 50p per unit. This doubles the price of cheap drinks such as cider and high-strength alcoholic drinks. It has been estimated that MUP will cut annual alcohol-related deaths by about 400.

Tackling poverty and poor health

The Scottish Government strategy to tackle income inequality and health inequality is set out in the 2008 *Equally Well Report*; an extract appears below:

Characteristics of policies more likely to be effective in reducing inequalities in health

- Structural changes in the environment (e.g. installing affordable heating in damp, cold houses)
- Legislative and regulatory controls (e.g. smoking bans in workplaces)
- Fiscal policies (e.g. increasing the price of tobacco and alcohol products)
- Reducing price barriers (e.g. free prescriptions)
- Starting young (e.g. prenatal and postnatal support and interventions, home visits to infants, good quality pre-school day care).

Overview of health improvements

The health of all citizens is improving, including those in areas of deprivation:

- The gap in life expectancy between the best and worst parts of the UK has fallen from 10.6 years to 10.3 for men and from 9.2 years to 8.1 years for women since 2000–2002.
- The death rate for heart disease and strokes in Scotland has fallen by over 40 per cent since 2005 and the cancer death rate is a third of what it was in 2000.
- The annual rate of child obesity has slightly decreased.

However, significant health inequalities still exist and NHS Scotland blames welfare cuts since 2010 for having a negative impact on the health of the poor. Coronary heart disease deaths in 45–74-year-olds are four times greater in the most deprived areas compared to the least deprived. A 2017 report by the Royal College of Paediatrics highlights the clear link between increased poverty as a result of welfare reforms and the increase in poor child health.

While numerous promotional campaigns to promote healthy living and preventative campaigns to detect cancer early have been successful, uptake has been far greater among the better off. This explains why men with prostate cancer and who live in deprived areas are nearly twice as likely to die from the illness as those in the more affluent areas. The figures for 2018 from the Detect Cancer Early (DCE) programme, which was launched by the Scottish Government in 2012, highlight this social inequality. In deprived areas over 30 per cent of people were not diagnosed until the later stages of cancer compared to only 18 per cent in the least deprived areas.

Government responses to social inequality

The Welfare State

The Welfare State is a product of post-war Britain and exists to provide social care from the cradle to the grave. The Labour Government implemented the principles of the Beveridge Report to provide a safety net for all citizens based on the main principles of equality and collectivism. The National Health Service was set up, state education expanded and a social security system introduced to protect elderly, disabled and unemployed people.

Beveridge's five 'giant evils' in society

- **Want:** A reformed social security system would provide every citizen with their basic financial needs.
- **Ignorance:** Education would be reformed so that every child would gain a worthwhile level of education.
- **Squalor:** A massive rebuilding of safer and progressive housing would ensure better living standards for all.
- **Idleness:** A reformed economic policy including the nationalisation of industries such as railways, gas and electricity would ensure low levels of unemployment.
- **Disease:** A new National Health Service that would be free at the point of entry would be created for everyone's health needs.

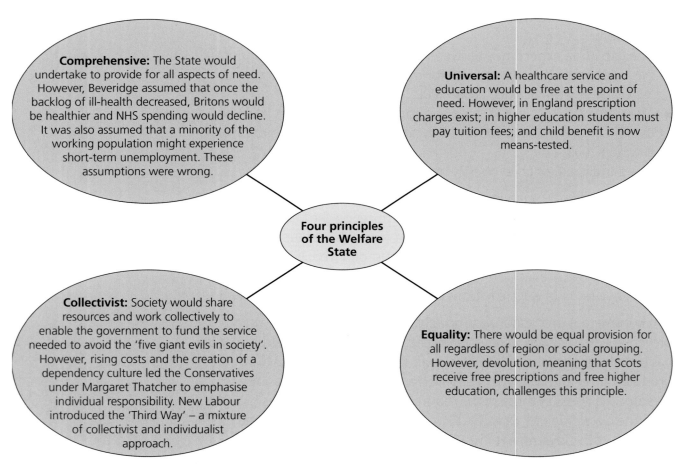

Comprehensive: The State would undertake to provide for all aspects of need. However, Beveridge assumed that once the backlog of ill-health decreased, Britons would be healthier and NHS spending would decline. It was also assumed that a minority of the working population might experience short-term unemployment. These assumptions were wrong.

Universal: A healthcare service and education would be free at the point of need. However, in England prescription charges exist; in higher education students must pay tuition fees; and child benefit is now means-tested.

Four principles of the Welfare State

Collectivist: Society would share resources and work collectively to enable the government to fund the service needed to avoid the 'five giant evils in society'. However, rising costs and the creation of a dependency culture led the Conservatives under Margaret Thatcher to emphasise individual responsibility. New Labour introduced the 'Third Way' – a mixture of collectivist and individualist approach.

Equality: There would be equal provision for all regardless of region or social grouping. However, devolution, meaning that Scots receive free prescriptions and free higher education, challenges this principle.

Figure 6.6 The four principles of the Welfare State

Strategies to increase levels of employment

From National Minimum Wage to Living Wage

The National Minimum Wage (NMW) was introduced in April 1999 and then rebranded in 2016 by the UK Conservative Government as the National Living Wage (NLW) for those over 25. In April 2019 the payment was £8.21 an hour. Around 1.8 million workers receive the NLW and it has helped to reduce the gender pay gap, as women account for about 60 per cent of low-paid jobs.

New Deal

The New Labour Government introduced the New Deal for Lone Parents (NDLP) as part of its package to address inequality in the UK. New Deal also has programmes for other groups including New Deal for Young People (NDYP), New Deal 25+ and New Deal 50. The New Deal ended in 2011.

Tax credits

The Labour Government of 1997 had a long-term goal to halve child poverty by 2010 and abolish it within a generation. Working tax credits and child tax credits were central to this strategy. The lower the income, the more tax credits individuals and families received. These credits were designed to tackle child poverty and help to ensure that work paid more than welfare. Since 2011, the number of individuals and families receiving credits and the amount received has been reduced.

Jobseeker's Allowance

The Jobseeker's Allowance was introduced in 1996 to replace Unemployment Benefit and is available for those seeking work. At the Jobcentre, a 'Claimant Commitment' is drawn up that sets out the steps that need to be taken to find work. If a claimant fails to carry out the details in the agreement then their benefits can be stopped.

Jobcentre Plus

Jobcentre Plus is a government agency that supports people of working age to move from welfare to work and helps employers to fill their vacancies; it also helps to provide opportunities for retraining and gaining more skills to increase the likelihood of people entering employment. The *Universal Jobsmatch* website is the busiest recruitment website in the UK, with up to 6 million hits per day. In addition to helping people find work, the website allows the government Department for Work and Pensions to track users' attempts to gain employment, and those claiming Jobseeker's Allowance can have their payments stopped if they are not sufficiently active.

Pension credit

Pension credit is a means-tested benefit for elderly people on low incomes, who may depend only on their state pension. All pensioners, regardless of income, receive the Winter Fuel Payment of £200 per household; however, the Cold Weather Payment is means-tested. A new state pension system was introduced in 2016.

Reasons for the Conservative Welfare Reforms, 2010–2018

Economic

The banking and economic crisis of 2008–2010 led to a massive increase in government debt. The welfare budget was no longer affordable: overall spending on benefits was three times bigger in real terms than it had been in the late 1970s. The decision was taken to make over £100 billion in public sector savings by 2018.

Public support

The Conservative slogan that the system should reward 'strivers not skivers' met with general approval.

Tackling the dependency culture

Those out of work represent a drain on public finances and so getting people into work and contributing to the economy was regarded as the best solution to reduce the public deficit. It was felt that individuals should take more responsibility for their actions and life outcomes.

Over-complicated system

The Conservative Governments are simplifying the system by amalgamating a number of working-age benefits and tax credits into one single monthly payment, called **Universal Credit**. The Government claims the changes will be cheaper to administer, improve incentives to work, reduce fraud and encourage those on benefits to display greater financial responsibility.

Encourage individual responsibility

Housing benefit, for example, will no longer be paid directly to the landlord but to the claimant as part of their Universal Credit monthly payment. The claimant will be expected to manage their budget and pay their landlord themselves.

> ### Key term
>
> **Universal Credit:** A new payment will simplify the benefits system by combining income-based Jobseeker's Allowance, Employment and Support Allowance, housing benefits and Working and Child Tax Credits into one monthly payment.

Factfile: Key welfare changes, 2013–2018

End of Child Benefit as a universal benefit

Families earning £60,000 or more on an individual salary no longer receive Child Benefit. This policy has been criticised for penalising stay-at-home mothers. A family with four children and one salary of £60,000 receive *no* Child Benefit. In contrast, a two-income family with a combined income of £100,000 still receive *full* Child Benefit!

End of the spare-room subsidy in Scotland

More commonly referred to as the 'bedroom tax', this policy was introduced to address some of the shortages of social housing. Its aim was to encourage those living in large houses to downsize and so reduce waiting times for larger families to find suitable accommodation. A reduction in housing benefit of 14 per cent for those with one spare bedroom and 25 per cent for those with two or more spare bedrooms has been implemented.

However, there is a shortage of available homes for people to move to and the reduction of benefits paid to vulnerable people in society has had a detrimental impact on their lives.

In May 2014 it was announced that the 'bedroom tax' would be scrapped in Scotland after the Coalition Government agreed to give Scottish ministers full powers to compensate the 70,000 Scottish households affected by this policy.

Universal Credit and Help to Work

Claimants who are unemployed for more than two years and who have been unsuccessful in the Work Programme will be enrolled in the Help to Work scheme and offered casual contracted work, also known as '**zero-hours contracts**'. Should a claimant refuse these offers without any good reason, they will incur financial penalties.

Personal Independence Payment and Work Capability Assessment

Previously known as the Disability Living Allowance (DLA), the Personal Independence Payment (PIP) is a payment given to people living with long-term illnesses or disabilities. The Work Capability Assessment (WCA) is applicable to anyone receiving Incapacity Benefit, Severe Disablement Allowance and Income Support paid on the grounds of illness or disability. Claimants will now be individually assessed, where previously they would only require a doctor's certificate. The assessments are carried out by a private firm. Between 2014 and 2016 over 200,000 people with a serious injury or disability were declared fit to work.

Figure 6.7 The introduction of Personal Independence Payment has had a distressing impact on many individuals living with disabilities

The Claimant Commitment and Work Programme

The Claimant Commitment replaces the Jobseeker's Agreement. Out-of-work people who break the agreed commitment face financial sanctions. In 2013 almost 900,000 sanctions were imposed on unemployed Scots. One man had his benefits reduced to £11 a week when he failed to attend an interview with a Work Programme, despite producing a doctor's certificate to say he had been diagnosed with terminal cancer and was not fit to travel.

The Work Programme requires those who have been unemployed for more than 12 months to enter on to a special programme in which private and voluntary companies, together with Jobcentre Plus, work to get claimants into long-term and sustained employment. This scheme replaces the New Deal and Pathways to Employment.

The Welfare Reform Act 2016

This set out to further reduce the welfare bill by £12 billion by 2020 and is impacting most on the poorest individuals and families in society as follows:

- The cap on the household incomes of workless families has been further reduced to £20,000 maximum per annum, or £23,000 if you live in London.

- Working-age benefits have been frozen until 2020.
- Low-income couples will no longer be able to claim the family element in tax credits – worth up to £545 a year for any third child born after April 2017. This also applies to child tax credits and child allowance.

The Scottish dimension

The SNP Government supports universal benefits and provides a collectivist, rather than an individualist, approach to the Welfare State. Universal Benefits such as free prescriptions and free eye tests exist in Scotland but not in England.

Since 2015 the Scottish Government has spent almost £400 million to soften the UK welfare cuts especially the 'bedroom tax'. Research by the Scottish Government estimates the annual UK social security spend in Scotland will have reduced to almost £4 billion by 2021.

New income tax and welfare powers

The new welfare and income tax powers granted to the Scottish Government mean that for the first time Scotland can develop its own social security system (see Table 6.3). It will, however, only be responsible for 15 per cent (£2.8 billion) of the present UK social security spending in Scotland. Nevertheless, it will introduce much less strict welfare rules, such as being paid twice rather than once monthly and not having benefits stopped for missing an appointment.

Table 6.3 Welfare powers in Scotland and the UK

Welfare powers granted to Scottish Parliament	Welfare powers retained by UK Government
<ul><li>Winter Fuel Payments</li><li>Cold Weather Payments</li><li>Personal Independence Payments (PIP)</li><li>Carer's and Attendance Allowance</li><li>Severe Disability Allowance (SDA)</li><li>Industrial Injuries Disability Benefits (IIDB)</li><li>Funeral Expenses Payment</li><li>Best Start Grant (formerly Sure Start Maternity Grant)</li><li>Discretionary housing payments</li></ul>	<ul><li>State pensions</li><li>Child Benefit and the following benefits now part of Universal Credit:<ul><li>Jobseeker's Allowance (JSA)</li><li>Employment Support Allowance (ESA)</li><li>Income Support (IS)</li><li>Working Tax Credits</li><li>Child Tax Credits</li><li>Housing Benefits</li></ul></li></ul>

New tax rates in Scotland

Scottish tax payers earning more than £33,000 a year will pay more tax than all other citizens of the UK. An individual earning £50,000 will pay £824 a year more in tax than someone with the same income outside Scotland. This extra revenue will be used by the Scottish Government to reduce social inequality.

Table 6.4 Tax bands in Scotland and the UK: 2018–2019

	Scotland	UK excluding Scotland
Starter rate	19% at £11,851–£13,850	no band
Basic rate	20% at £13,851–£24,000	20% at £11,851–£46,350
Intermediate rate	21% at £24,001–£43,430	no band
Higher rate	41% at £43,431–£150,000	40% at £46,351–£150,000
Additional/top rate	46% above £150,000	45% above £150,000

Social inequality: gender and ethnicity

Both women and people from ethnic minorities have made progress towards greater equality in the workplace through legislation and changing attitudes, but much has still to be done.

The glass ceiling

Despite more women going through higher education than men, women still lag behind men in income earnings and in promotion. The term 'glass ceiling' is used to describe how women and other disadvantaged groups are restricted in their ability to climb the promotion ladder; it usually refers to barriers to senior management. The Ambition and Gender at Work report by the Institute of Leadership and Management found that 73 per cent of women felt that barriers still exist for those seeking senior management and board-level positions.

Perhaps the biggest reason for a lack of women in top senior positions is the culture of 'presenteeism' that exists within UK businesses. Many senior managers are expected to work long hours. There is a real lack of flexible and part-time working arrangements in senior positions.

Hints & tips

In an exam on the effectiveness of government measures in tackling inequalities, you should be aware of the new welfare powers given to the Scottish Parliament.

Women and inequality

Women have lower pay

- Lower pay for the same work
- Work in lower-paid sectors of the economy
- Interrupted employment
- Part-time work.

Women take greater responsibility for family and caring

- Make up over 90 per cent of lone parents
- Bear a greater burden of the cost of children.

The gender pay gap varies from industry to industry, with the biggest differential being in banking and finance where men earn 42 per cent more than women.

Women are over-represented in areas of the economy that are low paid. Nearly two-thirds of women are employed in 12 occupation groups, sometimes described as the five Cs: caring, cashiering, catering, cleaning and clerical occupations.

Part-time work

Many more women than men work part time. Women are most likely to work part time when they are caring for young children. Approximately two-thirds of women with children under the age of 11 work part time, compared to only one-third of women with no dependent children.

The impact of government public sector cuts

One of the Coalition's economic policies was to reduce the number of public-sector workers while at the same time encouraging growth in the private sector. This strategy has had a detrimental impact on employment opportunities for women. The Fawcett Society and the Scottish Close the Gap project highlight that since 2010 three times as many women as men have become unemployed in the long term: 103,000 women compared to 37,000 men.

Lone parents

Perhaps the greatest reason that women face huge inequalities is the impact that being a lone parent has on employment. In the UK, 30 per cent of families are lone-parent families, which equates to 1.7 million parents with 2.9 million dependent children. Nine out of ten lone parents are lone mothers.

Figure 6.8 Lone-parent families are more likely to live in poverty than families with two parents

When lone parents find work it is often low paid, so they merely replace workless poverty with working poverty; lone parents have a high risk of living in poverty whether or not they are in work. According to research, nearly 86 per cent of working households that are in poverty are lone-parent households.

Progress and limitations

- Numbers of women are growing in occupations previously dominated by men. Women now account for 75 per cent of pharmacists, 40 per cent of medical practitioners, nearly half of all lawyers and almost 40 per cent of all accountants.
- In 2013, the Coalition Government announced new tax relief for families where both partners worked. Starting after the 2015 election, the Tax-Free Childcare scheme will cover 20 per cent of working families' childcare costs, up to £6000 per year and per child under 5. It will rise to cover children under 12 in subsequent years. This move is to encourage more women into work: currently 67 per cent of women work compared to 76 per cent of men.
- The gender pay gap has only slightly narrowed over the past 10 years. On average, for every pound a man earns, a woman receives only about 85 pence.

Ethnic minorities

According to the 2011 Census, the black and minority ethnic (BME) population is about 12 per cent of the total UK population. This figure has risen from 3 million in 1991 to about 7 million today. In Scotland, the minority population is 4 per cent of the total population. The BME community consists of a variety of groups, each of which has different experiences of wealth and poverty. In Scotland, the largest BME groups are Pakistani (30 per cent), Chinese (18 per cent) and Indian (16 per cent). A higher proportion of Bangladeshi, Pakistani and black non-Caribbean groups are living in poverty than any other groups.

Reasons for poverty in the BME communities

Low income and poor housing

It is estimated that around two-fifths of people from BME backgrounds live in low-income households – twice the rate of white British people. As a result, many live in poor housing in areas of deprivation. A significant number of individuals and families from a BME background lived in the Grenfell Tower. In 2017 a fire in the tower took the lives of 72 people.

Employment

In the past, many migrants had fewer qualifications or qualifications not recognised in the UK, so many were concentrated in low-paid industries such as hotels and catering. The youth unemployment rate for black people has increased at almost twice the rate for white 16- to 24-year-olds since the start of the recession in 2008. Young black men are the worst affected of all.

Culture

In 2017, 56% of Pakistani/Bangladeshi women were economically inactive, compared with 23% of Pakistani/Bangladeshi men (a gap of 33 percentage points), and 25% of white British women (a gap of 31 percentage points) (www.gov.uk). Traditionally, Muslim families tend to be larger and there has been a cultural expectation for women to stay at home in a caring capacity.

Poor educational attainment

This explanation has lost its veracity as in the last decade all ethnic groups have improved their average educational attainment. Indian and Bangladeshi students have been outperforming their white counterparts in achieving five A–C passes (or the numerical equivalents, which began to be introduced from 2017) in GCSE exams. However, barriers still remain, with many BME graduates working in non-graduate jobs – a staggering 41 per cent of African graduates fall into this category.

Discrimination

Race discrimination in the UK takes three forms: direct discrimination, indirect discrimination and institutional discrimination.

- **Direct discrimination** is when someone is denied an opportunity purely based on their race, ethnic origin, religion or belief.
- **Indirect discrimination** occurs when everyone has to conform to the same practice that would deny a certain group opportunities to practise their religion and celebrate their culture.
- **Institutional discrimination** occurs when an organisation's procedures and policies disadvantage people from ethnic minority backgrounds. It came to the fore in the Macpherson Report into the Metropolitan Police following the Stephen Lawrence Inquiry, where police attitudes to people from BME backgrounds were described as 'institutionally racist'; the police displayed racist stereotyping that disadvantaged minority ethnic people.

Since police began recording racist crimes in 2000 in Scotland, the number of incidents has risen by 75 per cent. Part of this increase may be explained by a greater willingness on the part of victims to report these crimes. However, a report by the Commission for Racial Equality Scotland stated, 'Verbal abuse … was so much a part of everyday life that most people did not think of reporting it.'

A lot of these attacks are concentrated in poorer and disadvantaged areas of cities where many people from BME backgrounds live. Therefore, many who are forced by low income to live in such areas become the target of racist abuse and violence. The perpetrators are mostly youths.

Government responses

- The Living Wage/National Minimum Wage, Working Tax Credit and Child Tax Credit have been used to increase the income of the lowest wage earners in society. As many female and ethnic minority workers suffer from low-income employment, these policies have been of particular benefit to these two groups.

- As women make up a larger proportion of pensioners, Pension Credit has helped improve the income of women who retire with reduced pension entitlement.
- The Equality Act 2010 brings together the previous nine pieces of equality legislation, including legislation covering gender, race and disability. The act gives women (and men) a right to equal pay for equal work, even if different roles are being carried out. The act also allows for positive discrimination: job adverts can be aimed at different ethnic groups or women if the organisation lacks representatives from that particular group. Finally, the act requires health organisations to eliminate discrimination in the provision of healthcare and thereby reduce health inequalities for BME groups, for example healthcare providers should be aware of the language needs of people living in their areas and provide health promotion in languages other than English.
- The Equality and Human Rights Commission (EHRC) safeguards the human rights of all citizens, especially designated groups. One important role of the EHRC is to monitor and report on pay divisions between the races and genders in unrepresentative public bodies.
- The Equality Act gives women a right to equal pay for equal work, even if different roles are being carried out. Women working for local councils involved in domestic duties such as catering have won discrimination awards against their employer.
- Companies with 250 or more workers have to publish information about the differences in men's and women's pay; the same applies for public bodies with 150 or more workers. The BBC carried out a gender gap audit which found a 9 per cent pay gap. It also highlighted that female BBC journalists, such as Carrie Gracie, the BBC China Editor, were paid less than men.
- The Scottish Government has a gender balance in the Scottish Cabinet and has set targets of a 50:50 gender balance on public sector bodies.

Responses from voluntary/charity groups

Voluntary groups play an important role in alleviating the impact of social inequality and acting as pressure groups to highlight the negative impact of UK government welfare reforms.

The Trussell Trust

This anti-poverty Christian charity provides emergency food and support to individuals and families. Over the last five years there has been a massive increase in the use of food banks. In 2017, over 1 million individuals and families received three-day emergency food supplies in over 400 food banks across the UK.

Source: The Trussell Trust

Chapter 7
Crime and the law

What you should know

To be successful in this section, you should know about:

★ the legal rights and responsibilities of UK citizens, with an emphasis on the Scottish legal system

★ the causes and theories of crime

★ the impact of crime on victims, offenders and their families

★ the social and economic impact of crime on wider society

★ the effectiveness of custodial and non-custodial responses to crime.

Legal rights and responsibilities

In a democracy we expect to live a peaceful and harmonious life and to have a range of legal rights that are balanced by our legal responsibilities. Within a democracy, laws define the range and limits of our individual freedoms. We have, for example, the right to property and we should respect the property of others; we have the right to free speech but not to incite religious or racial hatred. In previous decades when acts of terrorism in Britain were carried out by the IRA, and in the present day when the majority are carried out by Islamist extremist groups, we accept laws that give wide powers to our police and courts.

Both the UK and Scottish legal systems continually update our laws. We accept limitations on our actions to prevent a complete breakdown of law and order (anarchy). In Scotland, we might not like the fact that we are not able to smoke in public places or that we have stricter drink driving laws than in England, but we accept that if we break the laws of the land we are committing a crime. Many Scottish football fans feel aggrieved that they have been criminalised by a law they disagree with (see below).

The OBFTC Act

The Offensive Behaviour at Football and Threatening Communications (OBFTC) (Scotland) Act 2012 became law in December 2011 to further strengthen laws against bigotry. Acts at a football match that used threatening or abusive sectarian behaviour, including offensive singing or chanting, brought penalties that ranged from fixed penalty orders to an unlimited fine and five years in prison.

Tom Devine, a Scottish historian, stated that the legislation is 'likely to go down in history as the most illiberal and counterproductive act passed by our young parliament to date'.

$\Rightarrow$

⇒

In June 2017, the Labour MSP James Kelly introduced legislation to scrap the act and, with the support of the opposition parties, the minority SNP Government lost the vote and the OBFTC Act was repealed in April 2018.

Figure 7.1 Most football fans opposed the OBFTC Act

The Scottish criminal justice system

Scotland retained its own legal system after the Act of Union in 1707 and Scots law is still the system we use today. Most law and order issues have been devolved to the Scottish Parliament (terrorism is one of the exceptions) and new laws are continually being passed or considered. The Scottish Government, for example, lowered the drink-driving limit in December 2014.

The Crown Office and Procurator Fiscal Service

In Scotland it is the Crown Office and Procurator Fiscal Service (COPFS) that decides whether or not to charge and prosecute individuals. It is responsible for prosecuting criminals and investigating complaints against the police. In an average year, it handles almost 300,000 reports of offences. The COPFS is headed by the Lord Advocate who, alongside the Solicitor General, is the principal legal adviser to the Scottish Government. The most serious High Court prosecutions are conducted by the Lord Advocate himself. For other cases at the High Court, experienced solicitors called advocates depute carry out prosecutions.

How does the court system work in Scotland?

There are three types of court in Scotland that deal with different levels of offending:
- the High Court of Justiciary
- the Sheriff Courts
- Justice of the Peace Courts.

The High Court of Justiciary

The High Court is the supreme criminal court in Scotland and deals with the most serious of crimes. The High Court is presided over by the Lord Justice General and the Lord Justice Clerk and has a jury of 15 members of the public. The custodial sentencing powers of the High Court are unlimited. When dealing with crimes such as murder, statute dictates that life imprisonment is imposed. The High Court also deals with all criminal appeal cases. For all appeals, at least two judges will preside but this may increase to five in complex cases.

The Sheriff Courts

A sheriff, who is an experienced solicitor or advocate, presides over trials at a Sheriff Court. Most criminal and civil cases in Scotland are dealt with in a Sheriff Court. In **solemn criminal hearing procedures** a jury sits, while in **summary criminal hearing procedures** the sheriff decides whether the accused is innocent or guilty, and, if the latter, they will also decide on the appropriate sentence.

- For solemn cases, the maximum sentence available to a sheriff is five years' imprisonment and/or an unlimited fine.
- For summary cases, twelve months' imprisonment and/or a fine of up to £5000 is available.
- A guilty verdict can be referred to the High Court of the Justiciary for sentencing if the sheriff decides that the crime merits a more severe sentence.

Justice of the Peace Courts

A Justice of the Peace Court is a lay court where the Justice of the Peace (JP) is supported by a legally qualified clerk. The court deals with less serious cases, such as theft, drunk and disorderly and traffic offences. The maximum sentence that a JP may impose is 60 days' imprisonment or a fine not exceeding £2500. In Glasgow's JP Courts, legally qualified 'stipendiary magistrates' have the same powers as in Sheriff Courts.

Court of Session

The Court of Session is Scotland's supreme civil court and sits in Edinburgh. It is both a trial court and a court of appeal. Although most civil cases take place at Sheriff Court level, high-profile cases involving large companies or sizable sums of money are heard at the Court of Session, for example much of the legal wrangling centring on Rangers Football Club has been heard at the Court of Session.

UK Supreme Court

The creation of the UK Supreme Court in 2009 has led to accusations that it is undermining the independence and distinctiveness of the Scottish legal system. The Supreme Court is regarded as the UK's highest court and argues that it can judge Scottish appeals if the accused is appealing under European Court of Human Rights (ECHR) legislation. For example in 2011, Nat Fraser, who had been found guilty of murdering his wife in 2003, appealed to the UK Supreme Court. Its verdict was that he should be retried in the High Court in Edinburgh and in 2012 he was found guilty for a second time.

Key terms

Solemn criminal hearing procedures: Trials such as murder, rape or serious assault are conducted in the High Court of Justiciary or Sheriff Court with a judge and a jury. In Scotland, a jury of 15 decides on the verdict of cases and a simple majority is needed to determine the outcome of the verdict.

Summary criminal hearing procedures: Offences such as breach of the peace are heard in a Sheriff Court or a Justice of the Peace Court without a jury.

A June 2014 decision by the UK Supreme Court had serious implications for Scotland. The court ruled that a trial of suspected terrorists could be held in total secrecy on grounds of national security. This decision goes against the basic principle that justice must be seen to be done and undermines citizens' rights. If a similar trial were held in Scotland and Scottish judges refused to hold it in secret, the UK Government could appeal to the Supreme Court.

In 2018, the Supreme Court became involved in the dispute between the UK and Scottish Government over powers returning from the EU such as agriculture and fisheries.

Figure 7.2 Supreme Court judges

Verdicts in Scottish courts

There are three verdicts that a jury can arrive at in Scottish criminal courts:

Guilty

A 'guilty' verdict can lead to a wide range of sentencing options, such as prison or community service.

Not guilty

A 'not guilty' verdict means that the accused is found innocent and, until recently, could not be prosecuted again on that charge. However, following changes in England, a new **Double Jeopardy** (Scotland) Act 2011 allows a second trial if compelling new evidence emerges.

Not proven

A 'not proven' verdict is unique to Scotland. The accused is free to go but with the implication that they have escaped conviction *only* because of some doubt or lack of evidence. In 2012, MSP Michael McMahon launched a consultation into this verdict as he believes it is 'illogical, inconsistent and confusing'.

It is argued that jurors are confused by this verdict, and the high profile trial of John Wilson in 2011 seems to support this view. The jury of eight men and seven women decided that the charge against him of assaulting Neil Lennon, then Celtic FC manager, merited a verdict of 'not proven'. This was despite the accused's admission that he had, during the Hearts–Celtic match in May 2011, run at the Celtic dug-out, swore and lunged at Neil Lennon, and struck

> ### Key term
>
> **Double jeopardy:**
> The legal principle that prevents people being tried for the same crime twice.

him on the head. The incident had occurred at a televised match and so clear evidence of his guilt was available. He was found guilty of a lesser charge.

The Children's Hearings System

The Children's Hearings System is the care and justice system for Scotland's children and young people. A fundamental principle is that children who commit offences, and children who need care and protection, are dealt with in the same system – as these are often the same children.

At the heart of the system are Children's Reporters, who are based in local communities. Children and young people are referred to the Reporter from a number of sources, including police, social work, education and health. They are referred because some aspect of their life is giving cause for concern.

The Reporter investigates each referral and determines whether compulsory measures of intervention are required; if they are, a Children's Hearing will be held.

The Hearing consists of three panel members, who are all trained volunteers from the local community. The Hearing listens to the child's circumstances and then decides what measures are required. The child may need a particular type of treatment or intervention, or they may be placed with foster carers, or in a residential unit or secure accommodation. The Hearing may decide that the child should remain at home with support from other agencies, such as social work.

The Hearings System aims to ensure that the best interests of the child are met and that they receive the most appropriate intervention and support.

Figure 7.3 The Scottish Children's Reporter Administration logo

The Scottish Children's Reporter Administration (SCRA) is one of the agencies that has a responsibility for how the Children's Hearings System operates. Focused on children and young people most at risk, SCRA's role and purpose is to:

- make effective decisions about a need to refer a child to a Children's Hearing
- enable children and families to participate in Hearings
- provide suitable accommodation and facilities for Hearings.

Further information about SCRA can be found at www.scra.gov.uk.

Another of these agencies is Children's Hearings Scotland (CHS), a relatively new public body established by the Children's Hearings (Scotland) Act 2011. The act created the role of National Convener, to act as a voice for Scotland's 2500 volunteer panel members and to ensure they are consistently supported to a high standard. The act created CHS as a dedicated national body, to support the National Convener in the delivery of functions related to the recruitment, selection, appointment, training, retention and support of panel members. Further information about CHS and the Children's Hearings system can be found at www.chscotland.gov.uk.

Figure 7.4 The Children's Hearings Scotland logo

Key facts

A total of 13,240 children were referred to the Reporter in 2017–2018, compared to 17,950 in 2016–2017. Referrals are split into two broad Categories (please note that children can be referred more than once in the same year):

- 11,268 on non-offence (care and protection) grounds
- 3060 on offence grounds.

The most common ages for children and young people to be referred to the Reporter continues to be 14 and 15 years. This applies to both care and protection and offence grounds.

In 2017/18, 32,553 Children's Hearings were held across Scotland for 14,076 children and young people.

The number of children and young people with Child Protection Orders (CPOs) in 2017/18 was 619. Of the 619, 159 (25.7%) were aged under 20 days at the date of receipt and 312 (50.4%) were aged under two years.

At 31 March 2018, 9493 children and young people were subject to Compulsory Supervision Orders. This is 1.0% of all children and young people in Scotland.

Source: www.scra.gov.uk

Child protection

Hearings can make short-term decisions to address emergency and/or high-risk situations where measures have to be put in place immediately to protect children or address their behaviour. This may include Hearings arranged as a result of the sheriff granting a Child Protection Order (CPO). The granting of a CPO requires the child to be removed to (or kept in) a place of safety away from home. For this measure to be considered, a child must be at risk of significant harm.

More CPOs are granted for very young children, reflecting their greater vulnerability and requirement for immediate protection. Hearings can also make an Interim Compulsory Supervision Order if they are unable to make a final decision but have concerns about a child. It might say where the child must live or other conditions that must be followed.

Source: www.scra.gov.uk

Theories and causes of crime

Criminologists and sociologists have long considered the factors that lead to crime. They ask themselves whether some individuals are born evil (nature) or whether it is the environment they grow up in that makes them carry out criminal acts (nurture). This is referred to as the nature/nurture debate. Criminology is the scientific study of the nature, extent, causes and control of criminal behaviour in both the individual and in society. Two main theories of crime are:
- biological and psychological
- sociological.

Remember
You should provide a balanced answer which covers the debate over nature (biological and psychological) and nurture (sociological).

63

Biological and psychological theories

This theory of crime was very popular in the late nineteenth and early twentieth centuries. Criminologists such as Cesare Lombroso claimed to be able to identify criminals from bodily characteristics, such as high cheek bones, fat lips and large ears. Later supporters of the biological school highlighted aspects of intelligence, personality traits and chromosomes. Twins and adoption studies give some support to the view that genetics have important influences on criminal behaviour.

Evidence suggests a link between imprisonment and those with conditions such as ADHD and depression. A young person struggling to control their ADHD may fail first at home, then at school, next at work and then finally with the law.

Hans Eysenck, a British psychologist, claimed that psychological factors such as extraversion and neuroticism made a person more likely to commit criminal acts.

The popular press tends to label those who commit violent murders as 'evil'. One such example was the murder of toddler James Bulger in 1993 in Merseyside. Two ten-year-old boys, Robert Thompson and Jon Venables, were charged and found guilty of murder. According to the tabloid press they were 'sons of Satan'; however, their family backgrounds displayed classic risk factors, including a chaotic lifestyle, poverty, alcoholism, marital breakdown, neglect and bullying. Interestingly, since their release at the age of 18 with new identities, Robert Thompson has not been in any further trouble, while Jon Venables has since been convicted on several charges and has been in and out of prison.

Gender also impacts on criminal behaviour. Based on conviction statistics, if you are male, you are more likely to commit a crime; while if you are female, you are less likely to commit a crime (95 per cent of prisoners are male).

Sociological theories

The sociological theory states that the individual is shaped by their experiences within family, community and friendship groups and by their socio-economic status. As such, it is a complex combination of factors that leads people to commit crimes, for example the vast majority of people who suffer poverty will never commit a crime. However, for a young person, the influence of sustained poverty combined with poor upbringing and peer pressure may lead them down a path of offending.

Sociological theories of crime

Chicago School

Chicago School sociologists highlight the importance of the urban neighbourhood in explaining crime. Urban areas with high levels of deprivation often experience breakdown in the social structure and institutions such as family and school. This creates an environment ripe for deviant behaviour, which leads to hotspots of crime.

Strain Theory

American sociologist Robert Merton highlighted that most mainstream cultures, especially in the USA, are centred around the dreams of opportunity, prosperity and freedom. This 'American Dream' becomes an intoxicating cultural and psychological motivation. However, if the social structure of opportunities is unequal and leads to many in society being denied the dream, some will turn to crime to achieve or maintain wealth and status. Others drop into deviant subcultures such as gangs and urban homelessness.

The causes of crime

Economic factors/poverty

Although there is no direct link between poverty and crime, evidence would suggest that those who are poor may be tempted to commit crime. Those who experience social exclusion are more likely to suffer from alcohol/drug addition, poor mental health and homelessness. There is a clear link between social exclusion and crime.

Youth crime

Around 49 per cent of youth crime is attributable to those aged 18–21. The under-15s commit around one-third of crimes, with the remainder attributable to those aged 16–17. Young people are responsible for higher proportions of offences such as fire-raising (86 per cent of offences are committed by young people), vandalism (75 per cent), theft of motor vehicles (75 per cent), handling offensive weapons (59 per cent) and housebreaking (55 per cent). The media tend to demonise young people with comments such as 'feral youths stalking our streets'.

Young people are also associated with gang culture and the influence of peer pressure. Recent studies have found that up to 3500 young people between the ages of 11 and 23 have joined one of the 170 street gangs within Glasgow's borders. Gangs can be felt to offer protection, status, conformity, a sense of community and excitement.

Level of education

There is a link between poor educational attainment and committing crime. Those who leave school as a NEET (Not in Education, Employment or Training) find it difficult to go on and gain employment. Children who are excluded from school are at risk of drifting into a life of crime.

Alcohol and drugs

Alcohol abuse is linked to many crimes, especially violent crimes. Nearly half of all of Scotland's prisoners say that they were under the influence of alcohol at the time of their offence. As part of a long-term study (the GoWell Programme) linked to health and wellbeing, Glasgow University academics found that people living in an area with six alcohol outlets or more can expect crime rates twice as high as those in an area with only three.

Drugs account for 29 per cent of violent crimes. Drug abusers are more likely to commit crimes such as burglary and muggings to fund their habit. However, it is debatable whether drugs actually lead people to commit crimes or whether those who use drugs are predisposed to a life of crime.

Greed and white-collar crime

Individuals who engage in corruption to finance an extravagant lifestyle can be motivated by greed. Temptation and opportunity can explain fraudulent action between friends and within families. In July 2018, Bernard Houston, 53, was found guilty of embezzling over £150,000 from his new wife after she had suffered a brain aneurysm. Over a four-year period, he used the money to gamble and live the high life. He was sentenced to 27 months in jail. After the trial, it was disclosed that Houston – a former care home worker – had been jailed in 2006 for stealing £2800 from an 85-year-old with dementia. The problem with **white-collar crime** is that as it is non-violent, not obvious and, as it is rarely committed against one victim, very hard to detect and prove.

Hints & tips

If you are answering a question on the causes of crime, you can highlight the male/female difference as evidence to support the biological theory in your answer.

Key term

White-collar crime: When fraud, embezzlement or other illegal schemes are used, mainly in the financial sector.

The impact of crime on society

Crime can have a terrible impact on individuals and their community, placing many in a state of fear (as illustrated in the anti-rape march described over the page). There are also financial costs to crime: the criminal justice system is not cheap, and there are costs associated with police services, court services and punishments.

Groups most likely to be victims of crime

Those living in poverty

Those who live in poorer areas are twice as likely to be a victim of crime and are also most likely to be repeat victims.

Young people

Young people are more likely to be victims of violent crimes, such as muggings and assault. According to the Scottish Crime and Justice Survey 2017, 8.2 per cent of those aged 16 to 24 reported being victims of violent crime; the figure is only 1.9 per cent among those aged 45 to 59.

Elderly people

The charity Age UK found that almost half of people aged over 75 are too afraid to leave their homes after dark because they believe they would be subject to verbal abuse or muggings. In recent years, criminal gangs have targeted elderly people to attempt to trap them in financial scams.

Women

According to pressure group the Fawcett Society, at least one woman in four experiences domestic violence in her lifetime, and between one in eight and one in ten experiences it annually.

More than 5000 join anti-rape midnight protest

More than 5000 people have taken part in a peaceful protest in Glasgow's South Side, which circled around the area where a 24-year-old woman was raped in May 2014. The walk came about following four sexual assaults in the city in as many weeks.

Two Govanhill residents, Ashley Crossan and Amanda Johnston, organised These Streets Were Made For Walking as a 'show of solidarity in support of the victims of rape and a call to action'.

Adapted from an article by Martin Williams from *The Herald*, 10 June 2014

Figure 7.5 The group marching in protest

The impact of crime on the offender

Committing a crime and receiving a prison sentence can have huge personal consequences for offenders and their families. Once released, many convicted criminals find life extremely difficult:

- They may suffer unemployment or difficulty in finding work because of their criminal record.
- They could be homeless, having lost their homes while in prison.
- They may experience marital difficulties created by the stress of being away from their spouses, and perhaps by the separation from their children.
- Some families can experience a great deal of shame and embarrassment, be the target of bullying or revenge attacks and even be forced out of communities altogether.

The impact of crime on the community

High levels of crime may damage community spirit and result in less neighbourliness. It leads people to prefer to 'keep themselves to themselves' out of fear of harassment or becoming involved in arguments that may lead to a criminal act. Areas with high levels of crime often suffer from vandalism and graffiti, making them less desirable and potentially more dangerous (see below).

'RED-flagged' streets too dangerous for ambulance crew

In July 2018, a Conservative MSP obtained data that highlighted that thousands of addresses in Scotland had been designated as being too dangerous for an ambulance to attend without police protection. One in three of these addresses is to be found in areas of deprivation in Glasgow. The inevitable delay in ambulance staff attending could be a matter of life and death for those who fall seriously ill in these areas.

Some crimes can rally a community together, as illustrated by the June 2014 anti-rape march in Glasgow (see page 67). A further example was in Blantyre in 2011, when thousands of people from communities around Blantyre marched against the use of knives and in support of murdered teenager Reamonn Gormley's family.

The economic impact of crime

- Theft, such as shoplifting, has an economic impact on businesses.
- According to the Home Office National Fraud Authority, white collar crime costs the UK economy £73 billion a year.
- Identity fraud is estimated to cost the UK £5.4 billion a year.
- According to the Scottish Government, over £2.6 billion was budgeted for criminal justice in 2018–2019.

The political impact of crime

Public and media pressure can persuade the government to bring in new laws such as:

Sarah's Law

In 2000, an eight-year-old girl, Sarah Payne, was abducted and murdered by Roy Whiting, who had previously been convicted of abducting and indecently assaulting a young girl. The *News of the World* newspaper led a nationwide campaign for better protection. New laws in England and Scotland were set up so that parents and carers can request criminal records held by police for people who have access to children.

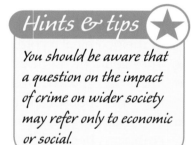

Hints & tips

You should be aware that a question on the impact of crime on wider society may refer only to economic or social.

Clare's Law

Following the murder of Clare Wood by her ex-partner, it was disclosed that he had a disturbing history of savage violence towards women. Her family and the media campaigned for greater disclosure, and in 2014 a new law in England and Wales allowed the police to disclose information on request about a partner's previous history of domestic violence or violent acts. The Scottish Government is considering its introduction.

The 2011 English riots

The Government's failure to prevent and control the 2011 riots that took place in London, Manchester, Birmingham, Bristol and Liverpool led to strong action being taken against the rioters. Five people died and 2500 shops and businesses were damaged or destroyed. One judge explained that such criminal behaviour 'must be met with sentences longer than they would be if the offences had been committed in isolation'. Those involved in the riots received sentences of up to two or three times longer than the normal term.

Figure 7.6 The London riots

The penal system

Figure 7.7 highlights that the action taken against those who commit crimes is not simply to punish but to deter and rehabilitate the criminal, thus reducing reoffending in the future. Many now question the effectiveness of a prison sentence for less serious crime and argue that alternatives to prison are more effective.

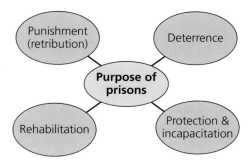

Figure 7.7 The purpose of imprisonment

Prisons work

- At any one time, over 90,000 UK criminals are locked up, thereby protecting the public.
- The victims of crime feel that justice has been done. The criminal is denied liberty and separated from family and friends.
- The possibility of a prison sentence deters individuals from committing crime.
- Prisons offer prisoners opportunities to receive treatment if they have drug or mental health issues.
- For violent crimes including murder, society must protect its citizens by imposing custodial sentences.

Prisons fail

- Many criminals go in and out of jail, never being deterred or reformed, but only ever being further criminalised: 75 per cent of short-term prisoners reoffend.
- Overcrowding in prisons limits the number of prisoners who can take part in educational and offending behaviour programmes; there is insufficient space on these programmes for all prisoners.
- Overcrowding can create violent and chaotic conditions and makes it difficult for prison officers to control abuse of drugs and acts of violence between prisoners.
- Around 70 per cent of prisoners have histories of poor mental health and/or drug problems.

Source: www.gov.uk

Scottish female prisoner statistics

- The proportion of female prisoners in Scotland has increased from 3.5 per cent of the prison population in 2000 to 5.7 per cent in 2017.
- 80 per cent of women in Cornton Vale Prison have mental health issues.
- Female prisoners are ten times more likely to self-harm than male prisoners.
- 71 per cent of women in Cornton Vale have used drugs before being sent to prison.
- 71 per cent of women in prison have no qualifications. This compares to 15 per cent of the general population.
- Since 2008, 32 babies have been born while their mother was in Cornton Vale.
- Some 16,500 children each year in Scotland are directly affected by parental imprisonment. Fifty per cent of children in care go on to receive custodial sentences.
- The Elish Angiolini Commission into the treatment of female prisoners called for fewer women to be sent to prison: 75 per cent of female prisoners receive sentences of six months or less and the reoffending rate of these short-term prisoners is 80 per cent. As a result, Cornton Vale has been closed and a separate 80-capacity prison is being built to house the most dangerous women prisoners. The remaining prisoners will be based in new regional units designed to prepare female prisoners for release. Each will have a mother-and-child area and children will be able to stay overnight. ⇨

⇒
Prison statistics

- In 2009 the number of Scottish prisoners passed 8000 for the first time.
- In January 2014, two Scottish Victorian prisons – HMP Peterhead and HMP Aberdeen – were closed. A new super-jail – HMP Grampian – opened in 2014.
- The total number of prisoners in England and Wales is 85,500 and in Scotland the average daily number in 2018 was about 7500.

Source: www.sps.gov.uk

Alternatives to prison

In January 2014, Lord Carloway, one of Scotland's most senior judges, argued that the penal system should concentrate more on rehabilitation and less on retribution, and that this would be in the interests of society. The use of fines, community payback orders and home-detention curfews are alternatives to prison sentences.

Arguments for and against alternatives to prison

Arguments for

- Sending a criminal to prison for a year costs a minimum of £30,000; tagging an offender costs about £2000. The average cost of a community payback order is around £2400, which is approximately half the cost of a two-month prison sentence.
- Alternatives to prison allow offenders to remain with their families and may prevent family break-up and children being put into care.
- The offender can make restitution for their crime by improving the community.
- Offenders avoid the stigma of imprisonment and the possibility of falling into bad company and criminal culture in prison.
- The reoffending rate is lower for offenders who receive a non-custodial sentence compared to those who are imprisoned.

Arguments against

- The public and media perception is that alternatives to prison are soft options and fail to punish the prisoner. Many victims feel that the offender has received nothing more than 'a slap on the wrist'.
- Enforcement and monitoring offenders can be a problem: according to figures published by the Scottish Prison Service in July 2018, the number of home-detention curfews is rising. In 2016–2017, 241 breaches were recorded and the figure in 2017–2018 was 300.
- Many offenders break home-detention curfews and commit crimes. The private companies that monitor curfews overcharge for the services they provide.
- It is time consuming and costly to take offenders before the courts for failure to comply with crime prevention orders.

Main alternatives to prison
Electronic monitoring or tagging

Electronic monitoring or tagging has been used to enforce the home-detention curfew since its introduction in 2006. The service is run by the private sector. SERCO, the private company that runs the service in England and Wales, overcharged the UK Government by over £20 million. In Scotland, the security service is provided by G4S and the contract in Scotland is worth £13 million over five years.

Community orders

A court can order between 80 and 300 hours of supervised work, which must be completed within six months of the date of sentence. The offender can carry out their sentence in their free time if they are in full- or part-time work. They are also encouraged to tackle any addiction issues: in 2017, over 1800 UK offenders were placed on community sentence orders that involved drug treatment.

Disposal order fines

The two main types of financial penalty are fines and compensation. This combines elements of:

- **retribution** – based on the seriousness of the crime
- **deterrence** – showing the offender that crime does not pay
- **reparation** – paying the victim or society back for harm done.

Early release of prisoners (parole)

Many prisoners accused of very serious crimes such as murder do not serve the recommended time in prison before parole is considered. John Wilson brutally stabbed to death his 17-year-old girlfriend in 2008 and in 2009 was sentenced to a minimum of 12 years. Yet in 2018 the parents of the murdered victim, Michelle Stewart, received a Scottish Prison Service letter indicating that Wilson had been approved to receive temporary release.

Part Four: International issues

This section of the book provides summary course notes for the International Issues area of study.

You will have studied one of the following topics as part of your Higher International Issues area of study:
- World Powers
- World Issues.

World Powers refer to members of the G20 organisation that represent more than 85 per cent of the world's economies. In this revision book, we will concentrate on the USA, China and South Africa.

In the World Issues section of the International Issues area of study we will concentrate on the causes, consequences and attempts at resolution of a particular world issue; in this case, development issues in Africa.

In question paper 1 (the extended response/essay section of the exam) you will answer either a 12-mark question or a 20-mark question.

Chapter 8

World powers: The United States of America

Introduction

The USA is the third largest country in the world (by area) and has a very diverse population of 326 million people. The main ethnic group in the USA is white, but there are also large populations of black Americans, Hispanic Americans and Asian or Pacific Islanders (APIs).

The USA's government is split on three main levels: local county, state and federal (national) level. Each of the 50 states has the power to make decisions on state matters and the federal government oversees all national laws and policies.

People

There are several main ethnic groups in the USA. Because of its long-standing reputation as the 'land of opportunity', many people have moved to the USA over the years to settle. According to the US Central Bureau, the main ethnic groups in 2017 were:

- **white**, who make up around 61 per cent of the population and are the dominant ethnic group
- **black/African American**, who make up around 13 per cent of the population and mainly live in the South
- **Hispanic/Latino**, who make up around 18 per cent of the population and tend to come from areas such as Mexico, Cuba and Puerto Rico – both legally and illegally
- **Asian**, who make up around 6 per cent of the population and predominately come from China, Korea and Japan, which are closer to the west coast of America
- **Native American**, who now only make up around 1 per cent of the population; they are the indigenous population of the USA.

Figure 8.1 The USA

The US political system

The USA was founded back in the 1780s, when the country gained its independence and the Constitution of the USA was written. This written Constitution outlines the US government's powers, its structure and the role of each of the three branches of the US government: the Legislative,

Executive and Judicial. The first ten amendments of the Constitution make up the Bill of Rights, which outlines the rights of all American citizens.

Rights and responsibilities

Table 8.1 Some of the rights and responsibilities of American citizens

Rights	Responsibilities
To vote	To participate in politics and choose the leaders
To run for office	To respect the views of other people and of other political parties
To free speech	To respect other opinions that differ from your own

Federal government

The federal government is made up of three main branches whose roles are outlined in the Constitution. The system is based on the **separation of powers**; the idea that in a democracy no one branch can have ultimate control or power to make decisions by themselves. This provides **checks and balances** on the US political system to ensure that actions carried out by the federal government are agreed by all three branches.

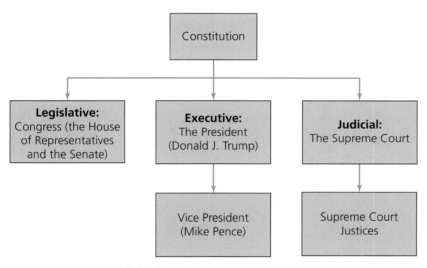

Figure 8.2 The national/federal government

Three branches

Legislative

Congress (the House of Representatives and the Senate) is responsible for making the laws or passing legislation. The Senate currently has 100 senators – two for each state. There are also 435 representatives in the House of Representatives, and the number of representatives from each state is based on the size of the state's population. For example, the State of California has the biggest population, so it has 53 representatives. Wyoming has a much smaller population, so therefore only has one representative. The composition of Congress changes every two years with the mid-term elections, which cover all of the House of Representatives and one-third of the Senate.

Key terms

Separation of powers: To ensure the American political system is as democratic as possible, the Constitution outlines how powers are separated between Congress, the president and the Supreme Court so that co-operation is needed between them before action can be taken.

Checks and balances: The three branches of the federal government (Congress, the president and the Supreme Court) all have the power to check each other: they can prevent one of the other branches from becoming too powerful by stopping them from taking a particular action. This means that power is balanced between the three branches because they have to agree with what the other branches are doing.

Executive

The president, vice president and cabinet are responsible for creating government policies. The president is also head of state.

Judicial

This branch is responsible for ensuring that all new laws to be passed by Congress, and actions to be made by the president, are constitutional. The president appoints judges to serve on the Supreme Court when a vacancy arises. The Court's role is extremely important: it ensures that the rights of Americans enshrined in the Constitution are protected.

Powers of the president

Many people regard the president of the United States as one of the most powerful people in the world. The USA is a democracy, however, and although Donald Trump has many important powers as president, there are also many important limits to his power. The three branches structure outlined on the previous page ensures that the president can never have ultimate control, and his actions are checked by both the Supreme Court and Congress. The president does still have the power to:

- **Suggest new policies:** he can suggest new policies that the government wants to put forward, for example President Trump's decision to tighten immigration laws (by removing DACA – Deferred Action for early Childhood Arrivals). These policies are often announced at the president's annual State of the Union Address to Congress and the American people.
- **Veto laws:** the use of the president's veto means that he can block or reject any law put forward by Congress to prevent it from being passed. However, Congress can overturn the veto if two-thirds of Congress vote to do so, and this usually happens when the Senate and the House of Representatives are controlled by the opposition party. Although there have been thousands of vetos enacted by presidents since 1789, Donald Trump has yet to use his while in power. Donald Trump did threaten to use his veto in March 2018 to block the US Congress' Budget Bill, but he was able to come to a $1.3 trillion deal with Congress over how the government should be funded.
- **Act as the US figurehead:** the president is responsible for appointing ambassadors and making treaties with other countries; he is also head of state. For example, Donald Trump has negotiated with other countries on the Paris Climate Change Agreement.
- **Command the armed forces:** the president is commander-in-chief (head) of the armed forces and can therefore order and mobilise troops and carry out military operations throughout the world. For example, in April 2018 President Trump ordered missile strikes on Syria because of suspected chemical weapon attacks.
- **Appoint justices:** the president has the power to appoint judges to the Supreme Court. For example in 2017 Trump nominated Neil Gorsuch to be the newest Supreme Court Judge (though his appointment had to be approved by the Senate).

- **Appoint his own cabinet:** the president has powers of patronage and can choose his own cabinet. Donald Trump has made several appointments to his cabinet after a number of high-profile resignations. For example, in April 2018 Trump appointed Mike Pompeo to become his new Secretary of State following the departure of Rex Tillerson.

Limits on the powers of the president

The Supreme Court and Congress check the powers of the president to ensure that they cannot become too powerful:

The Supreme Court limits the president's powers by:
- **deeming laws unconstitutional:** the Supreme Court can decide to reject any law if they believe it goes against the Constitution of the USA or the Bill of Rights; for example, in 2018, parts of President Trump's Travel Ban (which saw people from six predominately Muslim countries banned from entering the USA) was deemed unconstitutional by the Supreme Court because of 'religious discrimination'.

Congress limits the powers of the president by:
- **retaining the right to declare war:** only Congress can declare war on another country, even though the president is commander-in-chief of the armed forces
- **preventing presidential policies from progressing:** Congress can block any policies put forward by the president, and also decide the funds put towards each presidential policy; therefore, Congress can affect the success of presidential policies
- **overturning the president's veto:** although the president has the power to veto (reject) laws passed by Congress, Congress can overturn his veto with a two-thirds majority vote and the law will pass
- **impeaching the president:** this means that Congress can get rid of the president, again only with a two-thirds majority vote and by following the legal process; the real risk of this is very low – there have been only two attempts to impeach a president over the last 80 years: President Nixon and President Clinton
- **knocking back presidential nominations:** in April 2018, many Senators expressed a wish to reject Trump's nomination for Director of the Central Intelligence Agency (CIA) Gina Haspel, on the grounds that she was heavily involved in past CIA operations, which permitted the use of torture in order to facilitate confessions.

Other factors limiting the president's powers

The president is limited in the time they can serve as president; they can only serve a maximum of two four-year terms in office. This means that towards the end of a term, the president may struggle to implement policies and get backing for their proposals from Congress.

The composition of Congress can limit the president's power. Under the 115th Congress (2017–2019), both the House of Representatives and the

Senate are controlled by the **Republicans**. This enabled President Trump to have majority support in Congress. In the November 2018 mid-term elections, the Democrats regained control of the House but Republicans strengthened their control of the Senate.

Presidential election 2016

Donald J. Trump was elected to be president in November 2016 after defeating **Democrat** candidate Hillary Clinton. Trump's running mate and vice president was Mike Pence. Trump's election caused controversy as he failed to achieve as high a share of the popular vote as Hillary Clinton, but won the presidential election by achieving more electoral college votes. Many have argued that this is a flaw of the US electoral system.

Voting patterns and participation in politics

Ways of participating in politics

The American people can participate in politics in very similar ways to the British public. They can:

- stand for office (as a senator, governor or member of the House of Representatives)
- join a political party (Democrats or Republicans)
- campaign for presidential candidates (such as Jeb Bush or Hillary Clinton in 2016), senators or governors
- join interest groups such as the National Rifle Association (NRA)
- vote during local, state and national elections
- vote in state propositions (referenda).

Voting patterns in the USA

Voters are influenced on who they vote for by different factors, including income, geography, gender, race and party ideology:

- **geography:** those living in urban areas are more likely to vote for the Democrats. For example, 71 per cent of those living in urban Los Angeles voted for Democrat candidate Clinton in 2016.
- **ethnicity:** black Americans are much more likely to vote Democrat. A staggering 95 per cent of black voters voted for Obama in 2012 and 89 per cent of black voters voted for Clinton in 2016.
- **age:** younger voters are more likely to vote Democrat and older voters are more likely to vote Republican. Of the 18–44-year-old age group, 53 per cent voted for Democrat candidate Hillary Clinton in 2016, while only 39 per cent voted for Donald Trump. On the other hand, Trump attracted 52 per cent of voters aged 45 years and older and Hillary Clinton only attracted 44 per cent of this age group.
- **gender:** this became increasingly important in the 2016 election, possibly because of the controversy surrounding a number of sexual discrimination comments made by Donald Trump and also because of the high-profile campaign run by Hillary Clinton (who was seen as the candidate for women). Of female voters, 54 per cent voted for Hillary Clinton and 41 per cent voted for Donald Trump.

Key terms

Republicans: A political party associated with presidents such as Donald Trump. The Republicans tend to have more right-wing, individualist policies that reflect the ideas of capitalism and gun ownership.

Democrats: A political party associated with presidents such as Barack Obama (2008–2016) and candidates such as Hillary Clinton (in 2016). The Democrats tend to have more left-wing, collectivist policies that often benefit ethnic-minority groups and women.

Participation in elections

White people are still the ethnic group mostly likely to vote in presidential elections, although the influence of ethnic-minority groups during election time is increasing. Ethnic-minority voters are now more likely to turn out than ever because of:

- **education:** people from ethnic-minority backgrounds now have better access to education. Research (like that from the Center for American Progress's study 'Increasing Voter Participation in America' in July 2018) has shown that the more educated a person is, the more likely they are to understand the point of voting, and do so.
- **better representation:** there is a great improvement in ethnic-minority representation in Congress, particularly from black and Hispanic backgrounds; Obama standing as the first black presidential candidate meant increased registration to vote and increased turnout from ethnic-minority populations. The 115th Congress has set records as being the most ethnically and racially diverse in US history – one in five representatives is from an ethnic minority background, which encourages better racial minority political participation.
- **accessibility:** the Democrats and Republicans have tried to make voting more accessible in the Hispanic community by publishing their manifestos in Spanish as well as in English
- **high-profile celebrity campaigns:** campaigns by the likes of Beyoncé (in support of Hillary Clinton) and Kanye West (in support of Donald Trump) in 2016 are thought to have encouraged some ethnic-minority voters to see the importance of political participation. However, the percentage of black people voting fell from 66 per cent in 2012 to 60 per cent in 2016.

The influence of ethnic-minority voters during elections

Black and Hispanic voters in particular are playing an increasing part in the outcomes of presidential elections in the USA. This is because of:

- **population size:** it is thought that the Hispanic population alone will treble by 2050 due to higher birth rates and immigration; in 2016 people from ethnic minorities made up 31 per cent of voters, and there was a 17 per cent increase in eligible Hispanic voters between the 2012 and 2016 presidential elections
- **improved registration:** this is especially true in the black community; there are also 13 million Hispanic voters (although there are thought to be a further 8 million eligible voters who have not registered)
- **the influence of immigration in swing states:** the large ethnic-minority populations in states where no single candidate or party has overwhelming support, such as Texas and California, mean that these voters are particularly influential when it comes to the outcomes of elections; politicians often target campaigns to these areas during election times
- **traditional voting patterns among ethnic-minority communities:** Asian and Hispanic voters tend to be Democrat – 65 per cent of Asians and 66 per cent of Hispanics voted for Democrat candidate Clinton in 2016.

Immigration

The USA is an ethnically diverse country that was founded by immigrants. Millions of immigrants every year are attracted to the USA because of the American Dream. Immigration is, however, a highly controversial issue and recent governments have expanded their immigration control policies. Donald Trump in particular is keen on extending immigration control and made building a wall along the Mexican Border a key election promise. Today there is a debate between opponents of illegal immigration who are calling for tougher immigration controls and pro-immigration campaign groups who argue that immigrants are good for the economy.

Advantages of immigration

- The USA was built on immigration – immigrants bring culture and significant amounts of money to the US economy.
- In Texas and California especially, immigrants are vital to the economy. They provide cheap labour in the agricultural and hospitality sectors and keep the US economy competitive.
- In time, many immigrants earn increased wages and many are less dependent on welfare than native-born Americans.
- Many economists believe that immigrants contribute far more to the economy than they cost.

Disadvantages of immigration

- Some immigrants are uneducated and unskilled and are seen as a drain on health, welfare and education systems.
- Polls show that many Americans are in favour of tighter immigration controls, such as more border guards and high security fences.
- Areas populated by different ethnic groups often experience racial tension.
- Immigration has caused a lot of controversy in recent years with Donald Trump branding illegal immigrants 'animals' in a 2018 press conference. President Trump has tightened immigration laws by repealing DACA (see page 76) and increasing border security with plans to build a wall along the Mexican border.
- Before 9/11 immigration was an economic issue. Now it is perceived to be more of a security issue. Donald Trump's Muslim Travel Ban demonstrates this.

Social and economic inequalities

Although the USA is known as the 'Land of Opportunity', and it attracts millions of immigrants every year, its society is anything but equal. As a capitalist state with an economy based on boom and bust, there are always winners and losers. Anyone in America can suffer from poverty and lack opportunities, but unfortunately those from ethnic minority backgrounds (and black people and Hispanics especially) are still the most likely to suffer from poverty and to have lower income levels.

Poverty and income

In 2016, 8 per cent of white Americans lived below the poverty line. However, as research from the Henry J Kaiser Family Foundation reported, this figure is much higher among the black (21 per cent) and Hispanic (17 per cent) populations. Only 13 per cent of Cuban Hispanics live below the poverty line though.

In 2016, the median income for white Americans was $65,041, followed by $47,675 for Hispanic Americans and $39,490 for black Americans. Asian Americans are an economically successful ethnic minority group, earning on average $81,431 – much more than white Americans on average.

Healthcare

Americans from ethnic minority groups are more likely to be uninsured than white Americans. According to the US Census Bureau, 7 per cent of white Americans are uninsured, compared to 8 per cent of Asian, 11 per cent of black and 16 per cent of Hispanic Americans. Life expectancy for black and Hispanic Americans is three years less than among the white population: 75 years compared to 78 years.

Education

Graduation from high school rates show only a slight disparity between ethnic groups, with 96 per cent of white pupils graduating high school compared to 92 per cent of black high school pupils. The educational gap does, however, increase with the level of education. In 2017, 65 per cent of white Americans had a college level education compared to only 53 per cent of black Americans.

Housing

In 2017, the US Census Bureau estimated that 73 per cent of white Americans owned their own home compared to only 42 per cent of black people and 46 per cent of Hispanic people. In 2017, 7 per cent of white people lived in inadequate housing compared to 17 per cent of the black population.

Figure 8.3 The difference between rich and poor housing areas in the USA

Government responses to social and economic inequalities

In recent years the US Government has introduced a number of policies in an attempt to reduce social and economic inequalities:

- The Affordable Care Act (2010) – also known as 'Obamacare'
- Race to the Top (2014)
- Every Student Succeeds Act (ESSA) (2015)
- Tax Cuts and Jobs Act (2018).

The Affordable Care Act

The Affordable Care Act ('Obamacare') was introduced by the Obama administration in 2010. This Democrat policy aimed to ensure that all Americans had affordable health insurance and to improve the health of poorer Americans and those who were more likely to suffer as a result of expensive health cover (ethnic minorities, disabled people and those with pre-existing health conditions). It also expanded Medicaid for the elderly.

However, many Republicans were ideologically opposed to Obamacare and argued that it forced people to have health insurance, led to government interference in personal health matters and took away people's personal healthcare options. When Trump came to power in 2017, he vowed to dismantle Obamacare. Although Republicans failed to fully repeal Obamacare, Trump has made efforts to reduce its influence. He reduced administrative application support for Obamacare and reduced advertising for the programme by 90 per cent. Other measures ensured that people no longer have to pay for health insurance (removal of the individual mandate law). Although many Democrats and Republicans are in favour of this, stating that no one should be forced to have health insurance, some critics of the proposal argue that this could lead to 13 million more Americans becoming uninsured by 2027. Trump has also reduced spending on women's health issues, such as easier access to contraception and terminations – which were a key success of the Obamacare policy. Many people have argued that this change undermines women's human rights.

Race to the Top – Equity and Opportunity

This 2014 act introduced a fund of $300 million with the aim of:

- improving educational opportunities for all (government research around this time found that 54 per cent of people from the richest families completed college compared to only 8 per cent of those from poorer backgrounds)
- reducing expulsion and drop-out rates of ethnic minority children
- increasing attainment in inner-city schools
- increasing college affordability.

This act has seen some successes. Twenty-two million students and 1.5 million teachers in 40,000 schools received Race to the Top grants from the federal government which are thought to have helped to reduce high-school dropout rates. National Assessment scores in the states that have adopted the policy are the highest they have been in 20 years.

Every Student Succeeds Act

Signed by President Obama in 2015, this act aims to revise old education legislation (like the No Child Left Behind Act (NCLBA) 2002) and improve educational opportunities for all. This law transfers some educational policy power to states and allows them to focus funding where it is needed most. As part of the policy, students face standardised testing to ensure they are receiving high-quality education and this is recorded in league tables monitored by the federal government. The act also aims to focus additional funding on high-need students and underperforming schools. Crucially, it places emphasis on the expectation that students will go on to further education no matter what their income, race, gender or background. Every school is now to provide career education.

The policy is still in its infancy, but there have been some successes. This policy (along with previous laws such as NCLBA) have led to high-school graduation rates in the USA being at an all-time high, record levels of college enrolment and the lowest high-school dropout rates since records began. However, the policy is currently under review by the Trump administration. President Trump has been criticised for not prioritising education and the American Federation of Teachers have accused him of 'taking a meat cleaver to public education' because of proposed cuts of $9 billion to the federal education budget. President Trump has also removed an estimated $2 billion in funding available through the Federal Supplemental Educational Opportunity Grant Program, which is used to support low-income students through their college education.

Tax Cuts and Jobs Act

President Trump argues that this 2018 act will update America's outdated tax system, lead to more investment in business and allow entrepreneurs to create more jobs. The system has some winners – in particular, business people in the real estate sector who will be taxed less on earnings and when transferring property. It seems that big retail and technology companies (such as Google) will also benefit from the new corporate tax rate of 21 per cent (much lower than the 35 per cent rate some companies were paying previously). Advocates of the Republican's new policy argue that it will allow technology firms to reinvest and grow and will lead to America becoming more technologically innovative.

Staunch critics of the new policy argue that it will increase inequalities because the tax policy disproportionately benefits the rich. Millionaires will have to pay less inheritance tax and there are tax breaks for private schools. The act also works against the Affordable Care Act put in place by the Obama administration by getting rid of the fines that were imposed for people who did not have health insurance. It has been reported that, as a result of this, many people have dropped their healthcare plans (because they are no longer fined if they do not have health insurance) and this has increased the cost of health insurance

Hints & tips ★

Make sure that you can analyse how successful/ effective each of these policies has been in reducing both social and economic inequalities.

by an estimated 10 per cent. Also, the elderly have been hit by cuts to Medicare of around 4 per cent. However, in June 2018 President Trump had the highest approval rate of any president since records began, with around 41 per cent of American people approving of his policies.

The USA: power and international relations

Is the USA a superpower?

The USA is an extremely important world power and is widely acknowledged to be the biggest superpower. It has a huge population of 326 million people, the world's largest economy and unparalleled military might.

It also has 15 of the top 20 universities in the world, and is extremely technologically and economically advanced.

It plays a key role in international relations and co-operation and is a member of many international organisations, such as NATO, the United Nations (UN), the G7 and the G20.

The USA and the UN

The UN is an international organisation that was set up after the Second World War to encourage international co-operation and peacekeeping. It provides aid to developing countries and plays a major role in international security. The USA was a founding member and the UN headquarters are in New York.

The USA has one of the five permanent seats on the UN Security Council, along with China, France, Russia and the UK, meaning that it is always a key player in maintaining international security. It provides 28 per cent of the peacekeeping budget and co-operates with the other Security Council members to make decisions about world conflicts and intervention.

Case study: Conflict resolution in Syria

In 2018, Syria continues to be in the midst of horrific civil war, with many 'rebel' civilians fighting for their human rights against the tyrannical Assad regime. Other factions, including Jihadists, have also entered the conflict. In April 2018, the Assad regime in Syria was once again accused of using chemical weapons against its people – a breach of the Geneva Convention – which resulted in the deaths of an estimated 45 people. The USA, Britain and France were prepared to intervene militarily in Syria, arguing they had a moral duty to prevent the use of chemical weapons. However, Russia was against founding an investigation into the repeated use of chemical weapons, and failed to condemn the actions of the Assad regime. This led to tensions between the USA and Russia.

The USA, NATO and the G7

The North Atlantic Treaty Organization (NATO) is a political and military organisation that maintains international security and collective defence. It was founded in 1949, after the Second World War, and played a key role during the Cold War. Nowadays, the USA is a main player in the organisation, which has 29 member countries.

Increasing tensions between Russia and the USA (after Russia's 'illegal' annexation of Crimea in March 2014) led to Russia's expulsion from the G8. The result of this is an alliance referred to as the G7. International relations between countries change over time based on the diplomatic nature of their leader. When President Trump attended the Canadian G7 Summit in June 2018, he was accused of being aggressive and divisive over discussions on NATO funding. President Trump, a staunch critic of NATO, accused the UK and Germany of not paying enough into NATO military funding, insisting that the USA pays 'close to the entire cost of NATO'. He has vowed to see a fairer funding deal over NATO.

International diplomacy – USA and North Korea 2018

President Trump's approval rating reached an all-time high when he agreed to meet with North Korean leader Kim Jong-Un in Singapore in June 2018. The two countries had previously had an extremely hostile relationship after several highly publicised spats on Twitter in relation to military power and nuclear weapons. The meeting has been seen as the first step in improving diplomatic relations between the two countries. President Trump has agreed to stop military training exercises between US forces and South Korean troops (in South Korea) and Kim Jong-Un agreed verbally to reduced nuclear weapon testing. It remains to be seen how the relationship between the two countries will continue to progress.

Remember

It is important to critically assess the impact that the USA has on international relations — think about this in terms of 'positive' and 'negative' impact but also the type of impact, for example, economic, political or social.

Chapter 9
World powers: The People's Republic of China

What you should know

SQA requirements

To be successful in this section, you should know about:

★ China: its political system and process:
  ★ constitutional arrangements and the main institutions of government, including the power and role which each institution has and the impact this has on political decision-making
  ★ the political rights and responsibilities of citizens
  ★ opportunities for influencing the political process and the extent of democratic political participation
  ★ evaluating the political system and the extent of democratic influence and control
★ China: recent socio-economic issues:
  ★ the nature and extent of socio-economic inequalities and the main groups affected by this inequality
  ★ government responses to socio-economic issues
  ★ the effectiveness of government responses to socio-economic issues
★ the role of China in international relations:
  ★ involvement in international organisations
  ★ relationships with other countries
  ★ evaluating international influence and power.

Introduction

The People's Republic of China (PRC) is the fourth largest country in the world by land mass and has the largest population in the world: 1.4 billion people. The country has a very complex political, social and economic history and although its **ideology** is still communism, with strict government control and limited human rights, it has made huge steps towards becoming the fastest emerging capitalist economy in the world. The dominant ethnic group is the Han Chinese, who make up around 92 per cent of the population.

The country faces many challenges, such as rapid population growth, severe environmental pollution as a result of rapid industrialisation and maintaining the balance between economic freedom and political control.

> **Key term**
>
> **Ideology:** A set of political beliefs that guide the government of a country.

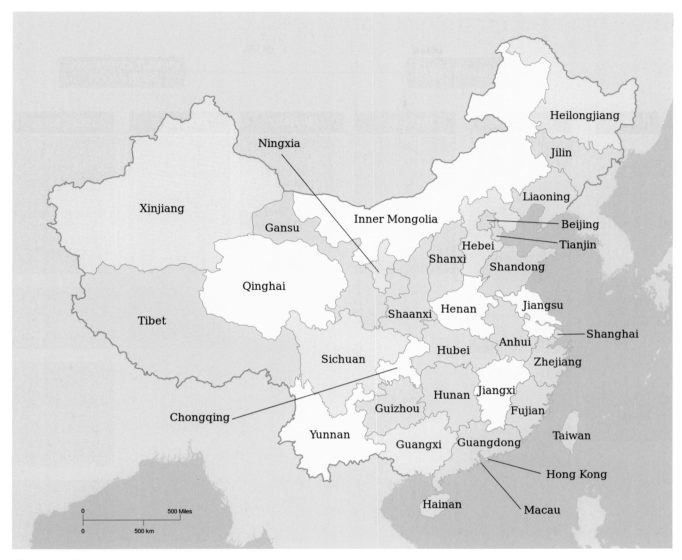

Figure 9.1 China

China's political system

China is run by the Chinese Communist Party (CCP) and has been since 1949. China is a one-party communist state with little political opposition. The government has strict controls on the population; it decides what people can access on the internet, what international politics they learn about in the classroom, what human rights they have and, up until recently, even how many children they can have. The CCP claims that true representative democracy is to be found not in Western human rights but in the people's responsibility and duty to the party and nation. As such, while the Chinese Constitution highlights the extensive range of rights of Chinese people, they can only be used in conjunction with the responsibilities of citizenship as defined by the CCP.

Figure 9.2 China's leaders: President Xi Jinping (right) and Premier Li Keqiang

The Chinese Communist Party

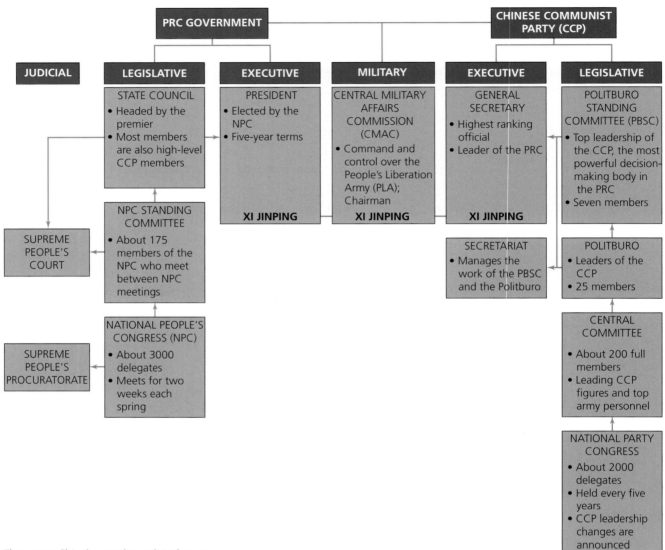

Figure 9.3 China's complex political structure

The CCP rules China from the top down under an authoritarian regime. In theory, anyone can apply to join the CCP, but in practice the membership process is competitive, rigorous and often only available to the elite or family members of current CCP members. To become a member, applicants must pass written applications, exams, interviews and a year's probation; this is all geared towards ensuring applicants' ideology matches that of the CCP and that they will be obedient to the party's beliefs. Membership is like a golden ticket to success in China; the connections and influence it provides allow better job prospects, healthcare and education for the whole family. There are currently 89 million members of the CCP (around 6.5 per cent of the population).

Many have criticised the CCP for not being representative of the population of China; there are very few women or people under 35 – although this is also the case for countries that are often viewed as more democratic than China (such as the USA and the UK). The CCP has a wide-spanning influence that dominates every aspect of people's lives: their choice of who to vote for, what they see on TV and the internet, which aspects of history and politics they learn in Chinese schools and also their rights.

The structure of the CCP is complex (see Figure 9.3 on page 88), but those at the top hold the real power. The General Secretary is Xi Jinping, who is also the country's president and military commissioner. Below him is the Politburo Standing Committee (PBSC) of seven members who act as the president's cabinet. This is where the main decisions for China are made – between the president and the PBSC. The head of the PBSC, and China's premier, is Li Keqiang. Underneath this level is the Politburo of 25 members (including the seven members of the PBSC).

National Party Congress of the CCP

Not to be confused with the National People's Congress (which is China's Parliament), the National Party Congress of the CCP meets once every five years. This is where major political decisions made by the CCP and the policies for China for the next five years are announced – the Five-Year Plan. It is also where members of the Politburo and PBSC are chosen.

The nineteenth National Party Congress took place in October 2017. Xi Jinping remained as the General Secretary of the CCP/president of China but there were some major overhauls. Five of the seven members of the PBSC retired and therefore five new members were selected – Li Zhanshu, Wang Yang, Wang Huning, Zhao Leji and Han Zheng. This signifies a huge change in leadership within the Politburo.

The Central Military Affairs Commission (CMAC)

In an authoritarian communist country, the army plays a vital role in national security and policing the nation. In China, the People's Liberation Army (PLA) has recently been needed to maintain order during protests in Tibet and Hong Kong. The CCP is permitted, by the Central Military Affairs Commission (CMAC), to control the PLA and China's nuclear weapons.

The CMAC has 11 members and it is their job to make decisions regarding army deployment, appointing high-ranking military personnel and arms spending. The CCP holds ultimate power over the CMAC, as Xi Jinping is also the Chairman of the CMAC. Xi Jinping announced in 2018 that the military is a key area for reform.

Is power shared?

The structure of the government

The Chinese political system is dominated by the CCP, although power is shared within the CCP more than it used to be:

Remember

The most important institutions of the CCP are:
☞ the Politburo Standing Committee
☞ the Politburo
☞ the Central Military Affairs Commission.

- Now there is a system of 'collective leadership' where Xi Jinping and the seven members of the PBSC have different powers and advisory roles. However, most decisions are made by Xi Jinping and in 2018 he removed the law stating that he could only serve two terms in power. This means he can serve indefinitely.
- There is a written constitution, which outlines people's rights, but it can only be used to further the interests of the state; that is, the CCP.
- The government structures – the State Council, Premier and National People's Congress – are controlled by the CCP top leadership.

Local politics

There are four levels of government administration: national, provincial, protectorate and county. The CCP dominates every level of government. People can vote in local village elections for the Village Committees.

Village Committees

Village Committees exist as the lowest level of government in China. Here, local people can vote for representatives and a chairperson, whose job it is to oversee local village decisions and provisions. They are elected every three years and 98 per cent of village committee representatives are directly elected by the people. It is real democratic progress in China to hold free, open elections with a secret ballot. However, there have been several criticisms of local elections, which have raised irregularities in the results and questions over how the votes have been counted. In Shanxi Province village elections in 2018, corruption was reportedly rife with candidates handing out cash, rice and oil in exchange for support. Also, the Village Committee is overseen by the Village Party Secretary from the CCP, meaning that even the Village Committees have to keep in line with CCP policy.

> **Remember**
>
> Only at local level can Chinese citizens vote for their representatives.

Political parties

On paper, China may appear to be a multi-party state, where people have a choice of different political views, but in practice this is not the case. Although eight minor 'democratic' political parties exist, they cannot be described as political opposition to the CCP, as views that differ from those of the CCP are not tolerated. Independent candidates are allowed to run in local village committee elections but they seldom make the ballot.

Anyone found to be starting a political party of their own faces prison or 're-education through labour'. Therefore, China can only really be considered as one-party state.

Case study: Human rights in China – Liu Xiaobo and Liu Xia

Liu Xiaobo was a very famous writer and political activist who fought for improved human rights and political reform in China. He initially rose to fame for his political writings around the time of the Tiananmen Square protests (1989) and campaigned throughout his life to end the one-party political system. Liu Xiaobo was arrested several times for his peaceful political protests and spent many years as a political prisoner in re-education labour camps, where he was tortured. He was eventually tried and detained indefinitely in 2009 for 'inciting subversion of state power'. His trial, however, was recognised as an international breach of human rights – he was not allowed to speak, was denied adequate political representation and neither the international press nor his wife were allowed to be present. His political activism and human rights work in China were recognised on a global scale when, in 2010, he was awarded the Nobel Peace Prize (which he never collected due to his detention). He died in hospital in 2017 having never been released from custody.

Liu Xia (Liu Xiaobo's wife) is also an avid political activist who continues to fight for improved political freedoms in China, even after her husband's incarceration. She was held under house arrest by the Chinese authorities after her husband was awarded the Nobel Peace Prize in 2010, even though the Chinese Government had never tried her with a crime. This meant that she was not free to leave her house unless accompanied and that she was not allowed visitors. She was eventually released from supervision and house arrest eight years later in 2018 and fled to Germany.

Case study: The cult of personality – Xi Jinping

Every leader has a different style of ruling, depending on both their personality and what their country's political system will allow. Political control in China has always been very tight and this has been made even more so by President Xi Jinping. Although it is written in the CCP's political charter that there will be no 'cult of personality' tolerated within the party, Xi Jinping seems to be in violation of this. He has cleverly used both media propaganda and political laws to ensure that his image is a positive one. He has also tried to maintain significant control over political matters by immersing himself in every branch of the Chinese political system.

In 2018, Xi Jinping's government changed the law to remove the limit on the term for which he can rule. Previously in China, the president could serve for only two terms (similar to the set up in the USA) but there is now no limit to the number of terms that a president in China can serve for. This means that Xi Jinping could theoretically rule for life (as previous leaders like Chairman Mao did). Western observers have also accused Xi of taking more control of the military and getting rid of many high-profile figures in China's civil service and legal courts under the vague banner of 'corruption'. Xi is in charge of the government, military and internet control, and is head of a reform committee looking into government corruption. Restrictions on internet use have also been tightened considerably under Xi, with certain phrases such as 'personality cult' being banned from retrieving results through internet search engines.

Political freedoms – Hong Kong

Until 1997, Hong Kong was a British colony. When it was handed back to China, it was to be ruled under the 'one country, two systems' formula. This meant that Hong Kong would be recognised as a Special Administrative Region which enjoyed many more political freedoms than the rest of China, but was still under Chinese control. This has led to many political challenges – Hong Kong is the fourth most densely populated area in the world, with incredible wealth. It is one of the most influential areas in the world for banking and finance and the most expensive place to own property in the world. There have been calls for Hong Kong's government officials to be fully democratically elected, but the Chinese authorities have tried to prevent this.

In 2014, tensions came to a head in high-profile protests after increasing political friction – the Chinese Government had been increasingly accused of trying to remove political and religious freedoms in the area so that it is more in line with the rest of China. Since 2014 an annual pro-democracy protest has taken place in Hong Kong in July; it was attended by 50,000 people in 2018.

China's economy

From 1949 to the mid-1980s, China was a rigid communist country where farmers worked under a commune system (state farms) controlled by the CCP.

We can describe this system as backward:
- People worked the land and earned a wage but had no incentive to work hard.
- This system severely limited food production, individual wealth and economic growth.

This system, therefore, was overhauled in the 1980s when Deng Xiaoping introduced agricultural reforms that allowed farmers greater economic freedom. Deng stated that 'to get rich is glorious' – an unfamiliar concept in a traditionally communist Chinese economy. Many farmers, able to farm their own land, became wealthy and food production increased. Deng Xiaoping opened up China to trading with the West through the Open Door Policy, and an economically backward China began to take advantage of world markets. It joined the World Trade Organization in 2001.

The move towards a socialist capitalist market

Today:
- China has the second largest economy in the world (behind the USA)
- China is becoming more capitalist, with a modern market economy rather than its traditional state-planned and -owned economy

- there has been a huge rise in the number of multi-millionaires in China and many Chinese people have amassed huge wealth, purchasing luxury goods with their high disposable incomes.

However, vast social and economic inequalities now exist.

Why is China so wealthy?

Foreign direct investment (FDI)

Thousands of British and American companies have invested in China and set up businesses there. China is now thought to be in the top five countries for attracting foreign investment and an appealing place to set up a business: tax breaks, a cheaper labour force, low building costs and a market of 1.4 billion people make an attractive package.

The 'factory of the world'

China still produces more products for export than any other country in the world (around $2 trillion worth a year), although its reputation as the factory of the world is beginning to reduce (due to cheaper labour appearing elsewhere in the world).

Special Economic Zones (SEZs)

First set up in 1979, SEZs are concentrated areas for businesses and factories. Rapid economic growth is prioritised to these key areas and businesses are incentivised to start up there. Perhaps the most successful is Shenzhen: a fishing village 30 years ago, it is now home to nearly 16 million people, exemplifying the sheer scale of economic development and migration in China.

World leader in technology

Companies like Apple have set up in China. It is estimated that 1 billion smartphones have been sold in this country alone. Many companies, however, are now moving to other countries like Vietnam where labour costs are lower.

Agriculture

China produces 21 per cent of the world's food.

Increase in income

The average income in China has risen 500 per cent since 2001. Disposable income rose 9 per cent from 2016 to 2017.

Challenges facing China's economy

The rapid industrial growth that China has undergone in recent years has had a profound social and economic impact on its population in several ways.

Migration

For the first time in its history, China's urban population now outnumbers its rural population, and millions of Chinese people migrate from rural to urban areas in search of job opportunities. Most of China's population now lives on the eastern seaboard, putting pressure on housing and the social services the country provides. In 2017, there were an estimated 287 million rural migrant workers in China.

Environmental damage

China is currently suffering environmentally and in terms of people's health as a result of its rapid economic expansion. According to the World Health Organization, the air quality in parts of China is considered 'hazardous' and 'unhealthy' and health ministers believe this is impacting on life expectancy in the country. China is responsible for over one-quarter of the world's greenhouse gas emissions.

Slowing economic growth rates

In 2012, China's annual economic growth rate was around 8 per cent, but this has fallen every year since and is sitting around the 6 per cent mark in 2018. Standards of living are not rising for everyone and there is still mass poverty in rural areas.

Social and economic inequalities

China's substantial economic revolution has led to the creation of a strong middle class (see page 95). Freer economic policy has meant that many Chinese people can start up their own businesses for the first time and can become wealthy. The number of billionaires in China has risen from 170 in 2015 to 476 in 2018. The increasing middle-class population has led to a greater disposable income and, as a result, there is a growing demand for luxury goods within China itself.

However, this economic boom has not been experienced equally by everyone. Many migrant workers, who move to urban areas in search of jobs, work extremely long hours for very little pay. China's movement towards capitalism has created one of the most unequal societies in the world. In 2018, President Xi Jinping said that social inequality was the 'principal contradiction facing Chinese society today'.

Employment and income

China's average income for 2017 was around 74,318 yuan per year per person (around £8711). The Government's overdevelopment and investment in the east of the country, while overlooking the development needs of the west of China, has led to unequal economic growth. Therefore, income levels and employment opportunities vary widely in different parts of the country. Those who live in rural areas have few job opportunities and still tend to work in the agricultural or mining sectors, both of which pay very poorly. According to recent World Bank data, more than 400 million people were living on $4 a day. Those who live in urban areas earn around three times as much as those in rural areas, and the attraction of the city pulls many migrants from rural to urban areas, especially to SEZs.

The 'floating population'

China's rural-to-urban economic migrants are often referred to as the 'floating population' as they have no fixed abode and divide their time between working in urban areas for most of the year and returning home for brief family visits. Around 287 million people from rural areas work in the cities. This floating population is expected to continue to grow at an alarming rate, with around 300 million additional people anticipated to move to urban areas in the next 30 years. This has created a number of social and economic problems in urban areas, such as overcrowding and a lack of affordable housing and social services.

The middle class

China's class structure has changed in recent years and there is now a larger middle class in China than ever before. This is because the move towards a capitalist economy has allowed:

- people to start their own businesses
- more jobs to be created in service industries such as telecommunications, insurance, banking and technology
- people to have a higher disposable income; that is, extra money to spend on luxuries.

The middle-class population in China tends to be categorised as those who have a university degree or a professional degree and an above-average income (researchers have estimated that, by 2022, this will be around 76 per cent of the urban population).

Healthcare

The healthcare system is reliant on a person having health insurance, which is usually paid for by individuals, often alongside employer contributions. As the system is insurance based, and therefore reliant on income, it has inherent inequalities. The system itself is run by the National Health and Family Planning Commission, which has a Bureau of Health in every province.

China's health problems

China's healthcare system faces many challenges that can be attributed to lifestyle choices brought on by higher incomes and economic growth:

- **Obesity:** A rise in disposable income and the increased consumption of fast food have meant that an estimated one in ten people in China now have type 2 diabetes and one in five people now have heart disease.
- **Smoking:** There are 300 million smokers in China and around one-third of the world's smokers live in China. This has an extremely adverse effect on the population's health, increasing the risk of cancers and strokes.

Source: World Health Organisation

Government responses to improve healthcare

Previous health programmes, such as Healthy China 2020, are now being updated. In 2016, the Chinese Government launched the Healthy China 2030 plan, which aims to:

- improve health indicators, increasing life expectancy across China to 79 years by 2030 and reducing infant mortality rates
- promote a healthy lifestyle by improving health education in primary schools and increasing physical activity
- improve health services by employing more doctors and increasing personal healthcare spending
- improve air quality to reduce premature deaths and lower hospitalisation for conditions such as asthma.

The 2030 plan is in its infancy, but previous plans such as China 2020 have had some impact. For the first time, the Chinese Government acknowledged the impact that environmental air pollution was having on people's health. New environmental monitoring has started to have an impact – China only experienced 23 heavily polluted days in 2017 compared to 58 in 2003. This has led to a reduction in hospitalisations for asthma attacks and lung disease.

However, the Chinese healthcare system is still flawed:

- Healthcare research funded by the Bill & Melinda Gates Foundation ranked it 92nd in the world.
- Patients have to pay for around one-third of their care and it is still one of the most unequal systems in the world.
- Corruption continues to be an issue, as many doctors are paid by the drug companies to prescribe unnecessary medication to their patients.
- China's health problems, for example obesity and type 2 diabetes, are increasing.

Education

Schooling in China is provided by the state, although private schools exist and are popular in wealthy, urban communities. China's education is internationally renowned and regarded as competitive and academically challenging. Everyone in China is supposed to receive nine years' mandatory education, although in reality this is not always the case, and once again disparities between rural and urban communities are very stark: while 80 per cent of urban students graduate from high school, only 20 per cent of rural students do so (also see page 97).

Government responses to improve education

China has the largest education system in the world – it currently educates around 260 million young people. The system does face many challenges, however, and is one of the most unequal in the world. There are large disparities between the standard of education received by children in rural areas, compared to those in urban areas. Also, China's huge migrant population means that there is pressure to ensure there are enough schools in urban areas. The Government has tried to improve education in China by doing the following:

- Improving pre-school education: the Government has made a commitment to universalising pre-school education by 2020. This would put an emphasis on improving literacy and numeracy – particularly in rural areas.
- Making the education system more equal: the Government has been increasing investment in rural schools, which tend to be poorly resourced. It has also tried to improve teacher recruitment in rural areas through the 'village teacher support programme' to ensure schools are fully staffed (at a cost of around 5.3 billion yuan). This programme has had some success – it has tripled the amount rural teachers are paid (in order to incentivise teachers to work there) and provided accommodation for teachers to live in.
- Increasing the emphasis on innovation and problem solving: the Chinese Government wants to ensure that Chinese citizens are fit for the workplace and this has led to a push on vocational skills and training.

Inherent inequalities do persist within the education system, particularly between rural and urban schools. Teachers in rural areas are given fewer training opportunities and fewer resources and it is estimated that around another 300,000 establishments would be needed in rural areas to meet the demand for high-quality pre-school education. Rural drop-out rates are far higher than those in urban areas, and very few rural teenagers go on to university compared to those living in urban areas. This is slowly improving, however, thanks to government quotas to encourage the enrolment of rural students at some universities.

Housing

Housing in China varies enormously, but the biggest deciding factor in the standard of housing a person lives in is personal wealth. There is an urban–rural divide to a certain degree, but those who live in the cities may also live in poor, substandard housing. Although those who live in rural areas are more likely to suffer substandard housing that may lack access even to electricity and water, urban life is no guarantee of decent housing: Many people now live in 'urban villages' which were once in the

Figure 9.4 Economically developed Shanghai

countryside, but have now been swallowed up on all sides by the emerging suburbs of ever-expanding cities. This engulfing of villages by cities leads to a disparity within the new urban area. Although the city has brand new buildings and apartments, the village attached to it is more like a slum or ghetto and becomes a breeding ground for crime and cheap migrant housing.

In comparison, wealthy citizens live in gated communities and expensive studio apartments. Their homes are designed for them and interior decorators are drafted in to create luxurious 'pads'. Beijing alone is home to 122,100 millionaires.

Government responses to improve housing

In 2017, the Ministry for Housing and Urban–Rural Development set several targets including the development of over two million new public homes with affordable rent. This is part of a trial scheme across 12 cities to boost the amount of good-quality, affordable housing. This continues to be a huge challenge for China, however, particularly in areas like Hong Kong.

Despite measures like this, China's housing system has the following problems:
- Mass migration continues to lead to a lack of affordable housing. Many migrant workers have no option but to rent rooms in 'urban villages', which are ghetto areas associated with crime and poor life chances.
- Rising house prices in areas such as Shanghai, which has seen house-price rises of over 600 per cent in the last decade. It continues to be hard for people to afford homes in the current global housing crisis faced by many developed countries.

Figure 9.5 Overcrowding in China's urban villages

Hints & tips

For 12- and 20-mark essays, make sure that you can analyse the effectiveness of government strategies to reduce social inequalities. For extra analysis think about whether the policy in question has been effective socially, economically or both.

Political rights in China

Chinese people have several political rights and responsibilities, as shown in Table 9.1.

Table 9.1 Political rights and responsibilities in China

Rights	Responsibilities
To vote in local village elections	To turn out to vote
To submit petitions to the Chinese government (the 2013 e-petitions website allows this)	To fill out their name, address and passport number for identification, to ensure names are not made up
To hold protests/demonstrations	To ask the permission of the government first and act peacefully
To join the CCP	To apply properly and follow the code of the CCP

According to the Freedom in the World Report 2017, China continues to be one of the least politically free places in the world to live. The CCP has very strict control over every aspect of life in China, leading countries like the UK to criticise China for its human rights record. The Chinese people have limited right to free speech, freedom of religion and political opposition, as ideas against CCP beliefs are not tolerated. New business opportunities and property rights are, however, beginning to give Chinese people more economic freedoms.

Internet control

It was widely reported that the number of internet users in China reached 800 million in 2018. This has led to:

- an increase in **cyber democracy**, where people anonymously post criticisms of the CCP; the CCP has responded by applying extreme methods of censorship
- the 'Great Firewall of China': the Government continues to ban Chinese people from accessing any websites that may be too 'westernised', for example BBC News, Amnesty International and Facebook, though there has been some relaxing of the 'Great Firewall' in areas like Hainan in an attempt to boost tourism and business
- the Government employing two million 'internet police' and paying bloggers to write articles that give a positive spin on the work of the CCP
- the continual monitoring of internet video platforms: Chinese people are unable to watch westernised shows like *The Big Bang Theory* and arrests over internet protests are common. In 2018, the Chinese Government blocked the viewing of Peppa Pig on the Douyin video website
- in 2017, the Chinese Government introducing regulations on 'collecting and using electronic data'. This allowed the authorities to collect and use private messaging such as texts, emails and social media posts to prosecute people for speaking out against the CCP.

Freedom of religion

According to Article 36 of the Constitution, Chinese citizens should have the right to practise their chosen religion. However:

- In 2016, the CCP held its first work conference since 2001 on the role of religion in China. The outcome was to agree stricter regulations and controls over places of worship.
- Xi Jinping has also called for a 'comprehensive management' of all religious organisations, which suggests that the CCP will be monitoring religious movements more closely in the future.

Human rights in Tibet and Xinjiang

Both of these parts of China are autonomous regions, but many people in these areas would like full independence from Chinese rule. The Chinese Government views Tibet as ruled from Beijing, but many people in the region wish to see Tibet as a free state. It is a similar case in Xinjiang where many Muslims in the area feel marginalised by Chinese rule and wish for

> **Key term**
>
> **Cyber democracy:** People using the internet to express their political opinions through channels such as social media and blogging.

independence for the region. This has led to several bloody uprisings, protests and up to 120 examples of self-immolation (setting oneself on fire in protest, leading to death) in Tibet.

Death penalty

China still executes more people every year than the rest of the world combined. The actual number of executions is never published by the Government, but it is estimated to be around about 5000 a year. A total of 53 crimes still carry the death penalty (although this has been reduced from 68) – something that has been widely criticised and condemned by nations around the world.

One-child policy

An improvement in human rights in China can be seen in the relaxing of the one-child policy. In fact, many people are now dubbing it the two-child policy. Now families can have:
- more than one child if either parent was an only child themselves
- a second child if the first is a girl if they live in rural areas, where restrictions are less strict.

The new policy saw 1.3 million more births in the year after the law was relaxed. Human rights issues do still exist, however; many people still face forced abortions, sterilisation and hefty fines for breaking family-planning rules.

China's international role

Is China a superpower?

Many people claim that China is an emerging superpower because it:
- has the world's largest population (1.4 billion people in 2018)
- has the second largest economy in the world (behind the USA) and is the world's largest exporter
- has a massive annual economic growth rate of 6 per cent per annum (although this has reduced from around 8 per cent in 2012)
- is a member of many key international **alliances**, such as the UN and the G20
- has a huge military spend of an estimated $171 billion (around one-third of USA military spending).

However, many people would not consider China to be a superpower as it lacks the military capabilities of other superpowers such as the USA.

China and the UN

The People's Republic of China has been a member of the UN since 1971 and plays a key role by:
- holding one of the five permanent seats on the UN Security Council (along with France, the UK, the USA and Russia)
- being an important part of UN agencies such as UNEP (the United Nations Environment Programme) and promising to reduce its carbon dioxide emissions

> **Key term**
>
> **Alliances:** An alliance is a group of countries that join together to achieve key economic, social or political goals. Examples include the G7, G20, UN, NATO and the EU. Alliances play a major role in international defence and economics.

- being a key economic contributor to the UN – China now donates the second highest amount to the UN's general budget and is the second highest contributor to the UN's peacekeeping budget
- providing assistance to fight international terrorist groups such as Boko Haram. China now supplies over 2500 peacekeeping forces around the world (compared to only five personnel in 1990).

China has had disputes with other countries, however, such as:
- territorial disagreements with the Philippines, Japan and Vietnam over areas of the South China Sea
- disagreement with France, the UK and the USA over the UN's action plan for Syria (Russia and China both continue to veto the plan which the other countries agreed should go ahead)
- growing economic frictions with the USA, with the USA imposing import taxes for Chinese goods such as solar panels and washing machines.

China and the G20

China is one of the main members of the Group of Twenty, or G20, countries. It has recently been heavily involved in:
- talks on how to solve the world financial crisis
- implementing measures to improve international economic stability.

As one of the richest countries in the world, China continues to dominate world economic affairs. However, China's relationships with other countries such as Germany continue to be lukewarm as a result of disagreements over how China conducts itself in terms of its political and human rights.

Relationships with other countries: China and the UK

Both Prime Minister Theresa May and Chancellor Philip Hammond have held high-profile talks with Chinese authorities for a number of reasons:
- The UK is looking to increase its business connections which China – especially post Brexit.
- Chinese engineers have helped create plans for a new nuclear power station at Hinkley Point in the UK.
- They hope to improve cultural links: there are now over 200 annual events that promote the UK's culture in China; also, the number of Chinese students in Scotland has risen to 7000.
- They hope to improve economic ties: the UK has benefited from economic ties with China; Scottish exports to China have now reached £500 million annually and over 1500 jobs have been created in Britain as a result of working alongside Chinese companies.

Case study: Chinese and American relations

In recent years, China has been keen to challenge US world dominance both economically and militarily.

Military power

Chinese military spending increased for the third year in a row in 2018 and rose to around 8 per cent. Total military spending in China in 2018 was thought to be around $175 billion, although this is still far behind the $700 billion US budget. Although Chinese military spending is thought to be behind the USA's spending, this is just an estimate. The Chinese authorities have been known to underplay their military spending and the Stockholm International Peace Research Institute estimates that the figure could actually be double the official Chinese government figure. China has also vowed to increase its spending on its nuclear capabilities and has created a new Rocket Force to review its missile arsenal. US President Trump, keen to show the US's military strength, stationed naval ships and airplane carriers in the South China Sea in 2018 – which was viewed as aggressive by Chinese authorities. President Trump also warned China against further militarisation in the South China Sea.

Economic power

While the USA may dominate militarily, it can be argued that China has the edge economically. Despite slowing economic growth, China is still the world's largest manufacturer and exporter of goods. Chinese exports were worth an estimated $2.2 trillion in 2017 in comparison with the USA's $1.6 trillion. China also provides considerable foreign loans to the USA: US debt to China is thought to be around $1.1 trillion. While the USA was badly hit by the 2008 economic crisis, China remained largely unscathed.

The USA has taken steps to protect its economy through recent economic policies. In 2018, President Trump promised to protect and prioritise American goods and jobs, and in June 2018, the US Government imposed new import tariffs on Chinese goods. Trump's policies introduced a 25 per cent import tax on goods such as electronics, airplane parts and manufacturing parts. The Chinese responded by imposing taxes on the US for Chinese foodstuffs, with the Chinese Government describing this as the 'biggest trade war' ever.

Chapter 10
World powers: The Republic of South Africa

What you should know

SQA requirements

To be successful in this section, you should know about:

★ South Africa: its political system and process:
  * constitutional arrangements and the main institutions of government
  * extent to which the political system allows democratic participation
  * political institutions and their ability to dominate government decision-making
★ South Africa: recent socio-economic issues:
  * the nature and extent of socio-economic issues
  * socio-economic inequality and its impact on a specific group in society
  * effectiveness of government responses to socio-economic inequality
★ the role of South Africa in international relations:
  * involvement in international organisations
  * relationship with other countries
  * evaluating South Africa's international influence and power.

Introduction

South Africa is a multiracial democracy based on a written constitution that includes a Bill of Rights. The country is a relatively new democracy as it was only in 1994 that the domination of the white minority ended (the apartheid system). In the first free multiracial elections, Nelson Mandela, leader of the African National Congress (ANC), became the first president of the new 'Rainbow Nation'.

South Africa is the richest country in southern Africa and the region's superpower. It is rich in natural resources and has a modern manufacturing industry, although the economic recession in the developed world has weakened its economy.

Figure 10.1 Nelson Mandela, father of the new South Africa, died in December 2013 and a nation mourned

Over 25 years on from the end of white rule, the **legacy of apartheid** remains, as indicated by the words of Archbishop Desmond Tutu in 1994:

'Apartheid has left a ghastly legacy. There is a horrendous housing shortage and high unemployment, healthcare is not easily affordable by the majority; Bantu [Black African] education has left us with a massive educational crisis; there is gross maldistribution of wealth.'

Unfortunately, for many poor black South Africans little has changed: high unemployment remains, education is still second class for many and the maldistribution of wealth is no longer between white and black but between the wealthy white and black elite and the people of the informal settlements, which includes poor white people.

Key term

Legacy of apartheid: The social and economic inequalities that still exist today between the races as a result of white rule (1948–1994) that separated the races (apartheid) and denied non-white people their political, social and economic rights.

Population

South Africa has a population of 56 million people made up of the following racial groups. Its citizens are referred to as the Rainbow Nation because of these racial groups and tribal identities (see Figure 10.2). There are 11 official languages.

Black African

Black Africans make up approximately 80 per cent of the population. The main tribal groups are Xhosa and Zulu. The black African population has increased from 74 per cent in 1994 to just over 80 per cent in 2017 due to a higher birth rate and white migration.

Coloured

The coloured ethnic group is made up of people who have multiple heritages. In South Africa, this tends to mean a shared black and white heritage. In the 2011 Census, this became the second largest ethnic group, overtaking the white population. Most people from this group live in the Northern and Western Cape. It is important to note that while the term 'coloured' is not acceptable in many countries, including the UK, it is used within South Africa to refer to this particular ethnic group.

White

The white population is declining and is now less than 9 per cent of the total population. White South Africans can be divided into two groups: English-speaking and Afrikaans-speaking. The Afrikaners ruled the country from 1948–1994 under the policy of apartheid. Many of the Afrikaners are farmers and regard themselves as the 'white tribe' of South Africa.

Asian

This population was brought to South Africa by the British in the nineteenth century and is the smallest racial group. Its population is about 1.4 million.

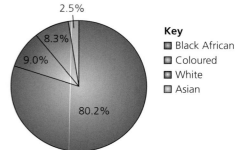

Key
- Black African
- Coloured
- White
- Asian

Figure 10.2 Population groupings in South Africa by percentage in 2017. Source: South African Government

Key political issues

To what extent is South Africa a successive and stable democracy, rather than a country moving towards being a one-party state?

South Africa: a political success story?

South Africa is a successive and stable democracy with free elections at all levels of government based on the Party List system of Proportional Representation. A free press exists and citizens can criticise actions of the government and join a political party, pressure group and/or a trade union.

The Constitution

South Africa has a written constitution that guarantees its people an extensive range of human rights. The constitution makes clear reference to the need to address the inequalities created by apartheid. Article 9.2 states:

'To promote achievement of equality, legislative and other measures designed to protect or advance categories of persons disadvantaged by unfair discrimination may be taken.'

This has enabled the ANC Government to pass legislation that discriminates against white people (see page 114), to further its goal of **Black Transformation**.

The constitution provides for an independent judiciary. The Constitutional Court is the highest court of the land, and deals with the interpretation, protection and enforcement of the constitution. One of its most famous decisions was to order the government of then President Mbeki to provide anti-HIV/AIDS drugs free of charge to mothers who have HIV/AIDS and their babies at birth.

Again, in 2017, the court defended democracy by ruling that MPs must be allowed to vote in secret. This was to enable ANC MPs to vote to remove President Zuma without fear of reprisal.

However, the dominance of the ANC has led to some critics stating that the country is moving towards a one-party state. Corruption is a major problem in South Africa. President Zuma was criticised for building a vast homestead that cost South African citizens R328 million (around £18 million).

Main institutions of government

South Africa has a bicameral parliament, consisting of a National Assembly (400 members) and the National Council of Provinces (NCOP). Elections for both houses are held every five years and are based on a system of Proportional Representation. The president is elected by the National Assembly from among its members and he/she is the executive head of state and also appoints the cabinet. The president may not serve more than two five-year terms in office. The dominance of the ANC ensures that the leader of the ANC becomes president.

> **Key term**
>
> **Black Transformation:** Government legislation to ensure that senior posts in the public and private sector and the allocation of government works contracts reflect the racial composition of South Africa.

'When he [Zuma] was elected President of the ANC (2007), he had more than 700 criminal cases – including corruption – hanging over his head. The charges were dropped by the NPA, which meant that not one of these cases was dismissed by a court of law ... With Zuma at the top, the ANC keeps the acronym but has acquired an unenviable image and different wording: Alleged National Criminal organisation.'

Extract from *The Fall of the ANC* by Prince Mashele and Mzukisi Qobo, 2014

South Africa is divided into nine provinces (see Figure 10.3), each with its own provincial government and premier. Eight of the nine provinces are controlled by the ANC and President Zuma used his power of patronage to appoint the respective eight premiers. The constitution offers limited powers to the provinces and their function is to implement the policies of the National Government. The Democratic Alliance, which controls the Western Cape, has been successful in delivering local services.

There are over 280 local councils, referred to as municipalities, and large cities such as Cape Town and Johannesburg have their own councils. Many councils are failing to deliver basic services such as refuse collection and school transport.

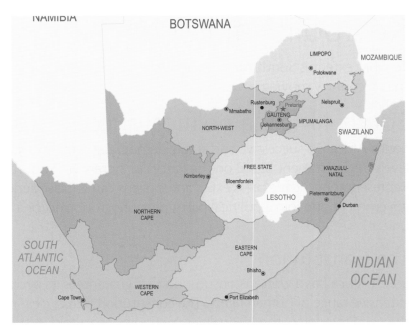

Figure 10.3 South Africa and its nine provinces

Participation opportunities

Apart from voting and being a member of a political party, South Africans can join pressure groups, including trade unions and community groups. One pressure group known as Section 27 took the Government to court for failing to deliver school textbooks. Unfortunately, many local groups have lost confidence in their politicians and resort to illegal protests that in many cases become violent. Virtually every day in South Africa a violent protest occurs, especially in the townships denied the amenities promised by the Government, for example residents in an informal settlement in Gauteng barricaded roads with burning tyres in protest at the lack of running water, electricity and sanitation. Many South Africans do not trust the police, and events such as the Marikana massacre of 2012 reinforce the view that official trade unions and the police are there to serve the ANC and not the people.

Political parties

African National Congress (ANC)

The ANC dominates South African politics and is the party of Nelson Mandela and black liberation. It has won all five of the national elections and, despite the cloud of corruption hanging over President Zuma, it won over 60 per cent of votes and 249 seats in 2014. Black African people, especially the poor and poorly educated, remain loyal to the ANC. In 2018, Zuma was forced to resign as president. In December 2017, Cyril Ramaphosa became the new leader of the ANC and 'persuaded' Zuma to resign his office. Ramaphosa was elected by Parliament to be the new president of the country.

National Freedom Party (NFP)

Zenele kaMagwaza-Msibi, former chairperson of Inkatha Freedom Party (IFP), set up the NFP in 2011 with other former IFP members, thus weakening the IFP. The NFP won six seats in the 2014 National Election and in the provincial elections in KwaZulu-Natal it gained six seats.

⇨

⇨
Democratic Alliance (DA)

The DA is the second largest party, with 89 seats, and in the 2014 National Election it retained control of the Western Cape. The DA has increased its support in every general election. Its main supporters come from the White, Coloured and Asian communities. It now has support of a growing number of black African voters and has a black leader, Mmusi Maimane.

ONE NATION. ONE FUTURE

Economic Freedom Fighters (EFF)

Julius Malema, the former ANC Youth leader, formed EFF in October 2013 and gained an impressive 6.4 per cent of the votes in the 2014 National Election. EFF won the support of the far left and young disillusioned black African voters. It advocates nationalisation of the mining sector and land redistribution without compensation.

Inkatha Freedom Party (IFP)

The IFP, led by Chief Buthelezi, draws its support largely from Zulu-speaking South Africans. It wants greater powers to be given to the provinces. It is a party in decline, and lost heavily to the ANC in the 2009 National Election in KwaZulu-Natal, and in the 2014 National Election the party only won ten seats.

United Democratic Movement (UDM)

The UDM was formed in 1997 and has witnessed a steady decline since the 1999 National Election. Its leader is a former member of the ANC, Bantu Holmisa. Its power base is the Eastern Cape, where it came third in the 2014 Provincial Elections. It won four seats in the National Election in 2014.

UNITED DEMOCRATIC MOVEMENT

Congress of the People (COPE)

This is a new political party, formed in 2008 by former Xhosa members of the ANC who had supported Thabo Mbeki. It came third in the 2009 National Election but failed to win enough support from black African voters to challenge the ANC. It is now a party divided and in decline, with only three MPs.

COPE
CONGRESS OF THE PEOPLE

Figure 10.4 In January 2018, the new ANC president, Cyril Ramaphosa, replaced Jacob Zuma as president of South Africa

Elections

National elections are held every five years under a Proportional Representation system, which closely matches votes to seats won by a political party. The formation of new parties is encouraged: four new political parties contested the 2014 National Election for the first time – NFP, EFF, Agang South Africa and African Independent Congress. This weakens opposition to the ANC as new parties divide the opposition. The use of a Party List system means that the loyalty of ANC MPs is to the party and not to the people, as there are no constituency links to the electorate.

Voter turnout of those registered to vote was a healthy 73.4 per cent in 2014, down from the 77.3 per cent of the 2009 National Election. However, these figures exclude the millions who failed to register. Only one-third of those aged 18 to 19 – the 'born-free' generation – voted.

The 2014 National Election

As expected, the ANC won the National Election with a clear majority – 62 per cent of the votes. However, it was the smallest percentage it has achieved in the five elections held since 1994, though the victory was still impressive and displayed the affection for Mandela's party by the black African population. Despite widespread ANC corruption, an economy with slow growth and massive unemployment, most black Africans voted with their hearts and not their heads. About 44 per cent of households depend on welfare payments to make ends meet, and the ANC has been criticised for using political rallies to give out state-funded food parcels to those who turn up.

The DA, with 22 per cent of the votes, achieved its best ever result, and more importantly it retained control of the Western Cape and significantly increased its support in Gauteng, gaining 30 per cent of the vote there. In total, the DA obtained over 4 million votes, compared to its previous high of just under 3 million in 2009. It is clear that the DA is widening its support to include educated and middle-class black African voters.

The EFF became the third largest party, with 25 MPs in the national Parliament. Significantly, it came second in two of the poorer provinces – Limpopo and North West. With a million votes, EFF hopes to win further support from unemployed and poverty-stricken citizens.

> ### Hints & tips ⭐
> You should be aware of both the strengths and the weaknesses of the South African PR Party List system. Can you list two advantages and two disadvantages of this system for the South African electorate?

> ### Remember 📌
> A popular exam questions is the political opportunities that exist for people to influence decision-making. As well as referring to specific examples from your world power, you should also consider the limitations of participation and influence.

A Challenge to the ANC

In 2015, the white leader of the DA, Helen Zille, resigned as party leader to be replaced by the party's first black leader Mmusi Maimane, who had been brought up in the black township of Soweto. The ANC had portrayed the DA as being a white party and stated that any black person who voted for them was a traitor. This is reflected in racial voting with only 6 per cent of black voters supporting the DA in the 2014 general election.

The DA's new image was reflected in the results of the 2016 local government elections. The ANC experienced its worst ever electoral result, winning only 54 per cent of the votes. In contrast, the DA won its highest ever with 27 per cent.

Internal party division within the DA and the removal of President Zuma (with accusations of corruption and unpopularity) have, however, weakened hopes of the DA winning over the support of a significant number of black voters.

Table 10.1 National Assembly election results for the main political parties: 2004, 2009 and 2014

Party	2004		2009		2014	
	Seats	Votes (%)	Seats	Votes (%)	Seats	Votes (%)
African National Congress	279	69.9	264	65.9	249	62.1
Democratic Alliance	50	12.6	67	16.7	89	22.2
Inkatha Freedom Party	28	6.9	18	4.5	10	2.4
Congress of the People	–	–	30	7.4	3	0.7
Economic Freedom Fighters	–	–	–	–	25	6.3

Source: Electoral Commission South Africa

To what extent is South Africa a successful democracy?

Table 10.2 Arguments for and against South Africa being a successful democracy

Arguments for	Arguments against
South Africa is a stable model of democracy for Africa. There have been five peaceful elections based on PR. In the 2014 National Election, 28 political parties participated, with 13 parties now sitting in the National Assembly.	There is a fear that South Africa is becoming a one-party state. The ANC has won all five post-apartheid elections convincingly and controls eight of the nine provinces. Only in Western Cape is it in opposition.
South Africa has a federal system of government, with powers divided between central and provincial governments.	The federal system exists only on paper. Provinces must implement the policies of the national government, such as BEE (Black Economic Empowerment) legislation.
South Africa has a liberal Constitution that guarantees freedom to its citizens. It provides for an independent judiciary. The Constitutional Court ordered Mbeki to provide drugs to combat HIV/AIDS.	The policy of transformation politics could threaten the independence of judges and the rights of non-black South Africans. Jacob Zuma regarded judges as 'arrogant' and ignoring the will of the people (the ANC).
There is a free press and civil society able to criticise and monitor the actions of the government. The success of the Truth and Reconciliation Commission highlights the openness of South African society.	The South African Broadcasting Corporation (SABC) is regarded as the mouthpiece of the ANC. In 2014 it refused to run DA and EFF political adverts as they criticised the ANC. A government 'Secrecy Bill' threatens the independence of the press.
A peaceful transition from Mandela to Mbeki occurred. Likewise, the power struggle between Thabo Mbeki and Jacob Zuma was resolved peacefully with the resignation of Mbeki as president in September 2008. Again in 2018, the new leader of the ANC, Cyril Ramaphosa, 'persuaded' President Zuma to resign.	There is an issue of corruption, with leading ANC members being sent to jail. President Zuma's vast homestead, built at the cost of R328 million (around £18 million) of taxpayers' money, highlights the arrogance and greed of ANC leaders.

Figure 10.5 Mmusi Maimane, the first black leader of the DA

Key events: the resignation of Jacob Zuma

August 2017 – The opposition parties' parliamentary vote of no confidence fails by only 24 votes to remove President Zuma from office – about 50 ANC MPs voted against their leader under the protection of a secret vote.

December 2017 – ANC delegates meet to elect a new leader of the party to become the new president of South Africa after the 2019 national elections. The two candidates for party leader are Cyril Ramaphosa, the deputy president, and the former wife of President Zuma, Nkosazana Dlamini-Zuma. A victory for Dlamini-Zuma will protect Zuma against corruption charges.

In a tense and vicious campaign, Ramaphosa wins a narrow victory and becomes the new ANC leader. He states that he will challenge corruption and provide moral renewal.

January 2018 – Supporters of Cyril Ramaphosa urge Zuma to resign as president. However, of the six top ANC leaders, three are loyal to Zuma, forcing Ramaphosa to move with caution.

February 2018 – Ramaphosa opens criminal investigations into claims of 'state capture' by the Gupta family (see below). Finally, faced with a vote of no confidence, Zuma announces on TV that he is resigning.

March 2018 – The new president, Cyril Ramaphosa, reopens the 783 counts of corruption against Jacob Zuma after a court rules that a decision to drop the charges a decade ago was 'irrational'.

April 2018 – Zuma appears before a court in Durban to answer corruption charges.

State capture

In 2016, a university independent report entitled 'Betrayal of the Promise: How South Africa is being stolen' accused Zuma and his key supporters of 'state capture' and of turning the country into 'a mafia-style fiefdom'. The report called on South Africans to 'defend the founding principles of democracy' and to work towards the removal of President Zuma.

The country's anti-corruption ombudsman responded by calling for a judicial inquiry into allegations that the Gupta brothers, tycoons and close friends of the Zuma clan, had influenced cabinet appointments and government contracts. It has been claimed that, under Zuma, corruption not only thrived, but was done in plain sight. Zuma, his family and his friends stand accused of looting state-owned enterprises and other public funds – it is estimated that they stole 20 billion rand (15 billion dollars), which could have improved schools, hospitals and housing.

One example of state capture was the discovery that 1.2 billion rand had been siphoned off from the Gauteng health budget over a five-year period (2010–2015). Only with the removal of Jacob Zuma is this crime now being investigated. In 2018, the Special Investigating Unit reopened the case against 12 ANC Gauteng politicians. Charges of corruption and maladministration have been made; for example, Brian Hlongwa, Chief Whip in the Gauteng Parliament, had bought a 7.2 million rand house with his share of the proceeds. This state capture resulted in massive debts for the Gauteng health service and resulted in significant cuts (see page 112).

Social and economic issues
Key issue
To what extent has the Government been successful in reducing social and economic inequalities?

Education

Problems

- The education system is still in crisis. The Swiss-based World Economic Forum ranks South Africa 146th out of 148 countries – and last in mathematics and science.

Figure 10.6 Many students drop out of school and fail to sit their exams

- Only four students in ten who begin school stay to pass the matriculation exams. In the Department of Basic Education's numeracy test, only 12 per cent of 12-year-olds scored above the minimum proficiency.
- Substantial inequalities exist between the provinces in terms of provision. In the Western Cape, 96 per cent of schools have electricity, whereas in the Eastern Cape that figure is only 60 per cent.
- Substantial inequalities exist between the provinces in terms of exam results. In Gauteng the pass rate is over 78 per cent, whereas in Limpopo it is 58 per cent.
- The schools with the poorest facilities and results are the schools in townships or rural communities. About 80 per cent of white children complete the final year of high school, compared to less than 40 per cent of black students.
- Standards of teaching are low, especially in maths and science. In a 2016 international comparison study in maths and science among 57 countries, South African students were place near the bottom. A staggering 27 per cent of pupils with six years of schooling cannot read compared to 4 per cent in Tanzania.
- The powerful South African Democratic Teachers Union (SADTU) is seen to have an unhealthy relationship with the ANC, and its union officials are not held to account for what many consider to be corrupt and incompetent actions. An academic report in 2016 found widespread corruption and abuse. This included teachers paying union officials for top posts.
- According to a 2018 report from the Department of Basic Education, more than 50,000 teachers at public schools are living with HIV and most of these teachers can be found in the poorer provinces of Mpumalanga and Eastern Cape.

Progress

- In 2016, the Government invested 21 per cent of its entire budget in education (6.4 per cent of GNP).
- Segregated education has ended and extra funding is given to poorer schools.
- Progress has been made in reducing to 40 per cent the number of schools with no sanitation, water or electricity.
- Black South Africans now make up 65 per cent of students in higher education.
- Grade 12 matriculation results (equivalent to the Scottish Higher) have improved significantly. In 1996 the pass rate was 48.9 per cent; by 2016 it had risen to 70 per cent.
- Free education has been expanded to enable students in poor urban and rural areas to attend school. Attendance figures increased

from 27 per cent in 2002 to 57 per cent in 2013. These same students receive a nutritional lunch (the 'Mandela sandwich').

- The number of adults with literacy problems has decreased. The *Kha Ri Gude Mass Literacy Campaign* involved more than 2 million people between 2009 and 2013.
- Higher education is now free for poorer students whose family income is less than 150,000 rand per annum.

Health

Problems

- A shortage of doctors and nurses places a strain on the health service.
- The HIV/AIDS epidemic has led to a decline in life expectancy, which had dropped from 62 in the 1980s to 52 in 2006.
- Provinces that recorded the highest HIV/AIDS prevalence were KwaZulu-Natal (37.4 per cent), Mpumalanga (36.7 per cent) and Free State (32.5 per cent). The Northern Cape and Western Cape recorded the lowest prevalence at 17.0 per cent and 18.2 per cent, respectively.
- UNAIDS estimated that around 7.1 million South Africans were living with HIV at the end of 2016, including 460,000 children under 15 years old.
- South Africa has the world's sixth largest tuberculosis (TB) epidemic, with a TB incidence rate of 438,000 in 2016 (60 per cent of people living with HIV are also co-infected with TB as their immune systems are weak).
- The health system was shamed in 2018 when it was disclosed that 143 mentally ill patients in Gauteng had died of thirst and hunger after they were removed from a well-run hospital and put into unregulated care homes.

Progress

- A free healthcare programme for children under six and pregnant women has been implemented.
- Immunisation against diseases such as polio and tuberculosis is free for all children under the age of six.
- Twelve state-of-the-art hospitals have been built.
- Availability of clean water to millions of South Africans has been a key weapon against illness and disease.
- Infant mortality rates have dropped from 58 to 29 deaths per 1000 live births between 2002 and 2015. This success is attributed to the availability of anti-HIV/AIDS drugs.
- A June 2018 report by UNAIDS highlights the progress that is now taking place in the treatment of the HIV virus. South Africa has the largest number of people – 3.2 million – on antiretroviral treatment (ART) programmes in the world.
- As a result of this ART programme, life expectancy has risen from 61.2 years in 2010 to 67.7 years in 2016.
- New infections have declined among South African children, from 25,000 in 2010 to 12,000 in 2016. This is mainly due to the success of the prevention of mother-to-child transmission (PMTCT) programme.

HIV/AIDS in South Africa in 2016

- 7.12 million people living with HIV
- 19 per cent adult HIV prevalence
- 270,000 new HIV infections
- 110,000 AIDS-related deaths
- 56 per cent of adults on antiretroviral treatment (ARTS) programmes
- 55 per cent of children on ARTS programmes

Source: UNAIDS, 2017

Housing and land

Problems

- The influx of rural populations to urban areas has led to the creation of thousands of informal black African settlements (squatter camps) that lack electricity and sanitation provision.
- Poor white people who lost their jobs under Black Economic Empowerment (BEE) legislation also live in squatter camps.
- Gauteng and North West have the largest numbers of informal settlements, with one in five of their citizens trapped in these poverty zones.
- Crime, unemployment and drug use are major problems in the townships and informal settlements.
- Regional inequalities still persist. Although 98 per cent of households in the Western Cape have access to piped water, this figure is only 60 per cent in Limpopo.
- For black African people trapped in informal settlements, racial segregation is still a reality.

Progress

- Since 1994, the Government has built over 4 million homes with access to electricity. Soweto is an example of a once-poor township of over a million people that now boasts a shopping mall and up-market housing.
- More than 90 per cent of households have access to running water and 85 per cent to electricity. Millions of South Africans who once lived isolated in darkness in forgotten black African communities have electricity.
- Around 80 per cent of households have a television, an electric stove and access to a mobile phone.
- Over 70,000 land distribution claims have been settled. Many black people prefer financial compensation rather than being offered land.
- Many different races now live in the same residential areas, reflecting the Rainbow Nation.

Wealth and employment

Problems

- The wealth gap has widened in South Africa since the enforcement of BEE legislation. The GINI coefficient, which measures inequality in society, was 0.59 in 1994; in 2018 it was 0.66. The top fifth of

Confiscation of white-owned land

Land reform since 1994 has been based on the willing-buyer-willing-seller principle, with compensation being provided. The Government target was to transfer 30 per cent of white-owned farmland to black people, but only about 10 per cent has been transferred. The radical political party EFF has urged the Government to nationalise the land and encourage poor black people to occupy white land. As a response, the ANC at its January 2018 conference passed a resolution to change the constitution and allow the Government to confiscate land without compensation. However, about two-thirds of South Africans live in cities and have no desire to return to the countryside.

the population earns 40 times more than the lowest and youth unemployment is running at 53 per cent.
- Unequal education creates unequal employment. The official unemployment rate among white people is 7 per cent compared to 30 per cent for black African people.
- Black African youth unemployment has risen to 50 per cent; white youth unemployment is about 15 per cent.
- A new term has been coined – tenderpreneurs – that refers to black African people who get rich from winning government contracts from politicians happy to accept cash for favours, which indicates that corruption is still rife.

Figure 10.7 The wealthy black elite are living luxurious lifestyles

Progress

- Thanks in part to affirmative action legislation, most black African people are better off than they were in 1994, either because of higher paid employment or because of the massive increase in welfare payments to the poor (social grants). The number who receive welfare grants has risen from 2.6 million to 16 million.
- The social grants system is the largest form of government support for people living in poverty. Most is given in the form of a child-support grant, which reached 8.2 million families in 2012 compared to only 80,000 in 2001.
- Between 1997 and 2014, the proportion living on less than $2 a day fell from 12 per cent to 5 per cent.
- The majority of black African people now have bank accounts, compared to one in five 20 years ago.
- Around 40 per cent of senior managers are now from the black African population, compared to about 4 per cent in 1994.

Affirmative action (positive discrimination) legislation

To achieve Black Transformation (see page 105), the Government uses positive discrimination legislation to set racial quotas for entry to higher education, public and private sector employment and the allocation of government contracts.

BEE legislation, including the Employment Equity Act, is enforced to ensure that employment, especially senior management posts, reflects the racial balance of society. This has led to the creation of a wealthy black middle class referred to as **Black Diamonds**. Many white people argue that reverse racism now exists. Critics of BEE legislation argue that it has helped only a small group of black African people while the majority have seen limited benefits.

Crime and the law

The fear and impact of crime is one issue that unites all races. The defence offered by the famous athlete Oscar Pistorius for shooting dead his

Key term

Black Diamonds: This new black elite of over 3 million now fills top posts in the public and private sectors. They live in the wealthiest suburbs of South Africa's cities beside their white neighbours. Their children go to the best state schools or to private schools and they have private health insurance to ensure the best medical treatment.

girlfriend in 2013 – that there was an intruder in his bathroom – is an occurrence feared by all.

Despite the official murder rate falling from an average of 55 a day to 44, South Africa still has one of the highest murder rates in the world. The Democratic Alliance claims that many crimes are not reported to the police as the public have little faith in the culprits being apprehended; police corruption and brutality are also major issues, with the last three National Police Commissioners being arrested on charges of corruption or fired for incompetence. The investigation into the Marikana massacre (34 striking miners were shot dead by the police) raised issues that the police had a shoot-to-kill directive towards the striking miners.

Why is crime so high in South Africa?

- It could be argued that the legacy of apartheid has created a culture of violence with easy access to guns. There is often a lack of respect and trust by the public towards the police. It has been claimed that appointments to top police posts are generally not based on ability or experience but on 'cronyism' within the ANC.
- The vast inequalities in wealth and the abject poverty within the informal settlements have fuelled criminal behaviour. Conviction rates, especially for rape, are very low. In a 2017 report, researchers found that of 500 sexual assault cases reported to the police in Diepsloot since 2013 only one resulted in conviction.
- The massive influx of poor people from the countryside to the towns and the arrival of 4 million illegal immigrants has created a group in society that ignores its laws. It is claimed that white farmers are more likely to be murdered than the average South African. The AfriForum, an Afrikaner pressure group, claim that this rate is 156 per 100,000.
- The Government has significantly increased police budgets and points to the reduction in crime, especially crimes of murder. By 2016, the murder rate had fallen to 34 per 100,000 of population compared to 44 per 100,000 in 2010 – although in 2017 there was a slight increase in the murder rate to 44.1 per 100,000 (see Table 10.3).

Table 10.3 Murder rates in South Africa, 2017 (selected provinces and national average per 100,000)

Eastern Cape	55.9
Western Cape	51.7
Limpopo	14.2
South Africa	34.1

Source: Africa Check, via South African Police Service

Key issue

To what extent does South Africa have influence in international relations?

South Africa and international influence

South Africa is an active member of the United Nations. The country was elected in 2006 and in 2010 by the UN General Assembly to serve on the Security Council. South Africa's role has been criticised by the West for placing its loyalties with the countries of the developing world ahead of human rights issues. In particular, a 'no' security vote on a resolution criticising the Burmese Government, and South Africa's original intention to vote against economic sanctions to be imposed on Iran, attracted widespread criticism.

Under President Zuma, South Africa's international human rights image has been tarnished. In 2016, when the Dalai Lama was invited to attend a meeting of Nobel peace laureates in South Africa, the Government refused him a visa. Yet President Zuma welcomed Omar al-Bashir, the president of Sudan, who has been accused by the International Criminal Court (ICC) of orchestrating genocide in the Darfur region of South Africa.

South Africa is the only country in sub-Saharan Africa to be a member of the G20, and the only African nation to have hosted the football World Cup finals, which took place in 2010.

Under the apartheid era (1948–1990), South Africa experienced international isolation. Following the abolition of apartheid, the stature of Nelson Mandela ensured that the new South Africa would play a leading role among the countries of the developing world and in international organisations such as the African Union and NEPAD (New Partnership for Africa's Development). Nkosazana Dlamini-Zuma, a leading member of the ANC in South Africa, was elected chairwoman of the **African Union (AU)**, highlighting South Africa's influence in the organisation.

South Africa has played a central role in seeking to end various African conflicts in Burundi, Democratic Republic of the Congo, Comoros and, more controversially, in Zimbabwe.

South Africa is a member of the BRICS (Brazil, Russia, India, China and South Africa) bloc, and is playing an important role in the shifting and distribution of power internationally. The BRICS bloc represents 43 per cent of the world's population and approximately one-fifth of global gross domestic product (GDP). South Africa sees its role in BRICS as promoting the African agenda. As President Jacob Zuma stated: 'Our belief is that the membership of South Africa to BRICS represents the 1 billion people on the continent of Africa.'

South Africa's active role as an independent country not afraid to challenge American foreign policy decisions has created diplomatic conflict with the USA. President Trump has threatened to cut funding to South Africa as it is one of the countries in the United Nations most likely to vote against the USA (it is among the top ten countries that are least likely to vote with the USA). In 2016, USAID foreign assistance to South Africa amounted to US$460 million.

South Africa – a regional superpower?

With one-third of the GDP of sub-Saharan Africa and two-thirds of that of the Southern African Development Community (SADC), the South African economy is the driving force of southern African development. However, Nigeria is now challenging South Africa's economic dominance. In April 2014, under revised GDP figures, Nigeria passed South Africa to become the biggest economy in Africa. Although, based on population size, South Africa's GDP per capita is way above Nigeria's (see Table 10.4), in August 2014 the South African economy was classified as in recession. Nigeria's internal problems, such as the Islamist militant group Boko Haram, have exposed the weakness of the Nigerian Government and division in society.

> ### Key term
>
> **African Union (AU):** A union consisting of 54 African states whose role is to provide 'African solutions to African problems', to support economic growth and to achieve conflict resolutions between states.

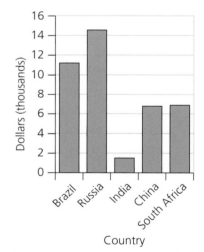

Figure 10.8 BRICS countries' GDP per head, 2014

Table 10.4 Nigeria and South Africa: GDP growth and GDP per capita, 2014

	Nigeria	South Africa
GDP growth	6.0%	2.5–3.0%
GDP per capita	$2800	$8000

World issues: Development in Africa

Defining development

A developed country is a country that can well look after itself; it has a strong, stable government, citizens can access social services such as education and healthcare and it is financially stable due to fair trade. People in a developed country can live long, healthy lives and better themselves through education, employment and social mobility. However, this is not the case for all countries around the world, and while countries such as the UK and the USA are well-developed nations, other countries in areas such as Africa are still developing.

Africa the continent

Africa is a continent of 54 countries and, like any continent, there are areas that are rich and others that are poor. The continent suffers from various problems that affect its development, many of which stem from its time of colonialism, when many African countries were owned by other nations. These other developed nations often used the African country's vast mineral and food resources and left them under-developed and politically inexperienced. There are about 1.3 billion people in Africa and in 2018, 23 of the top 30 poorest countries were in Africa. Each African country is different, and has its own political, social and economic challenges. Most though are blighted by poverty due to a combination of many factors – poor governance, debt, lack of social services, war, terrorism and poor economic relationships with other developed countries.

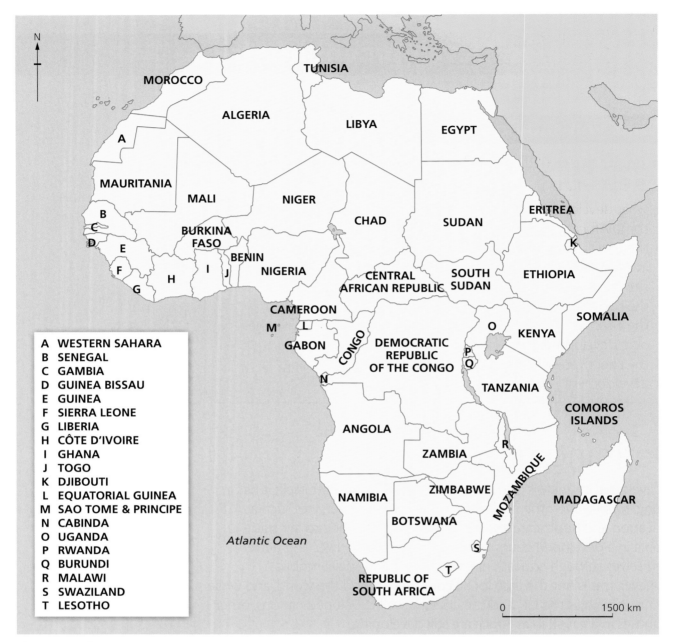

A WESTERN SAHARA
B SENEGAL
C GAMBIA
D GUINEA BISSAU
E GUINEA
F SIERRA LEONE
G LIBERIA
H CÔTE D'IVOIRE
I GHANA
J TOGO
K DJIBOUTI
L EQUATORIAL GUINEA
M SAO TOME & PRINCIPE
N CABINDA
O UGANDA
P RWANDA
Q BURUNDI
R MALAWI
S SWAZILAND
T LESOTHO

Figure 11.1 Africa

Measuring development

Development can be measured by development indicators, which are used to show a country's social and economic progress (see Table 11.1).

A high infant mortality rate (IMR) can show a lot about a country's healthcare system or access to basic healthcare. In African countries, healthcare provisions are often too expensive for people to afford or are badly under-resourced, leading to a higher IMR. Low literacy rates show that access to education is poor or that the quality of education received is sub-standard.

Table 11.1 Development indicators: developed and developing countries

Developed country	Developing country
Low infant mortality rate	High infant mortality rate
High literacy rate	Low literacy rate
Low birth rate	High birth rate
High levels of primary school attendance	Low levels of primary school attendance

Remember

Remember to analyse in your essays how social, political and economic factors are linked. For example, lower literacy rates (a social factor) can be caused by political factors such as conflict or terrorism, because children cannot go to school in war-torn areas. In some areas, lack of education (a social factor) can result from not having enough money to pay school fees (an economic factor).

Factors hindering development

Many countries in Africa suffer from a combination of social, economic and political factors that hinder overall development. These can include those shown in Table 11.2.

Table 11.2 Factors that influence development in Africa

Social	Economic	Political
Lack of healthcare	Cash crops	Conflict
Poor access to education	Trade	Bad government/kleptocracy/corruption

Although these factors can be identified separately as social, economic or political, they are all interlinked, and one issue tends to have a knock-on effect on the others, for example dictatorship or bad government can lead to a lack of social services like healthcare.

Healthcare in Africa

Africa is rife with health problems such as malaria, cholera and HIV/AIDS. Although drugs are available to treat malaria and suppress HIV/AIDS, they are not readily available to people and they are too expensive for most families to afford. Hospitals tend to be poorly resourced and staffed and they are in cities too far away from people living in towns or rural areas. In Liberia, for example, there are estimated to be around ten doctors per million people. To put this into perspective, in developed nations like the UK there are around 3000 doctors per million people. Liberia has also suffered from severe health problems in recent years – an estimated 5000 people died in Liberia during an Ebola outbreak in 2016. Other conditions such as HIV/AIDS affect millions of Africans each day – over 70 per cent of people infected with HIV/AIDS in the world live in Africa, and the World Health Organization estimates that 26 million people in Africa have HIV/AIDS. It kills 1.5 million people in that continent every year; that is 6300 a day. This has a huge impact on African society as it dramatically lowers life expectancy and prevents people from working the land or receiving an education.

Case study: HIV/AIDS in Swaziland

Swaziland has the highest prevalence of HIV/AIDS of any country in the world. Over 27 per cent of the population is HIV positive and this is severely affecting development in the region. There are over 81,000 orphans in the country who have lost their parents to the disease. The virus disproportionately hits women, with 31 per cent of women in the country having HIV/AIDS compared to 20 per cent of men. This is thought to be because of the sex-trade and high levels of sexual violence against women within the country.

The disease has dramatically reduced the number of farmers in the area, as it often affects people of working age, and this has reduced agricultural output. It is thought that the illness may kill up to 17 per cent of the country's farmers, making food shortages a real likelihood.

The transmission of HIV has been an ongoing issue partly because there is little access to sexual health information and contraception. However, there have been some steps forward – according to the WHO many more Africans are now being tested for HIV and there is an increase in the number of people infected with HIV gaining access to antiretroviral treatment to suppress their condition. The UN has set the ambitious 90-90-90 target by year 2020 in relation to HIV – the idea is that 90 per cent of people with HIV will know they have it (have been tested), 90 per cent of those who test positive will have access to antiretroviral treatment to help manage their condition and 90 per cent of people will be in control of their condition.

Case study: Malaria

In 2017, 91 per cent of the world's malaria deaths occurred in Africa.

Work carried out by the WHO, NGOs and other forms of aid has led to a 20 per cent reduction in malaria cases between 2010 and 2017. This has included providing medication, anti-mosquito sprays and mosquito nets.

Anti-malaria sprays have been applied to houses in some areas of countries such as Uganda, and this is 80 per cent effective in combating malaria. This has, however, caused problems for farmers in the area who specialise in growing organic fruit and vegetables. Exposure to the anti-malaria chemicals means that the farmers' fruit and vegetables can no longer be classified as organic and therefore the farmers lose sales as foreign markets will no longer buy their produce. The economic effect on farmers must be weighed up against the positive effects of reducing the spread of malaria.

Overall the impact of malaria on Africa's economy is estimated to be around $13 billion annually.

Access to education in Africa

It has long been acknowledged that educating a nation is the key to ending the poverty cycle. Better education allows for more job prospects and social mobility. It also improves technology, encourages innovation and helps to improve health knowledge and family education. Access to adequate primary education is, however, an ongoing issue in many African countries.

According to the World Development Report, which compares literacy and numeracy rates across the world, less than 7 per cent of primary school students in Africa show a competent level of reading ability. In countries such as Chad and Uganda, the drop-out rates are as high as 72 per cent and 68 per cent, respectively. Research from the World Bank also shows that countries in the north of Africa, like Tunisia, which have faced conflict in recent years, lag behind in key subjects like mathematics. It is estimated that it would take another 180 years, at the current rate of progress, for pupils in Tunisia to have an adequate level of numeracy.

Case study: African education statistics

- According to UNESCO (United Nations Educational, Scientific and Cultural Organization), 18 per cent of male and 24 per cent of female African children receive no primary education (2017). Primary school enrolment across Africa has increased over the last 15 years by 20 per cent, however.
- There is a stark gender gap – for every 100 male students out of school in North Africa, there are 132 female students (2017).
- Around 60 per cent of 15–17-year-olds are NEETS (not in education, employment or training).
- In Africa, only around 25 per cent of pre-school teachers and 50 per cent of secondary teachers have any formal qualifications and training.

Cash crops, economy and trade

African economies are growing – something which is often overlooked. However, this economic growth disproportionately benefits the rich and there is still a huge number of poor Africans who rely on trade with developed countries. Africa's rapid population growth of nearly 3 per cent a year also takes its toll on social services and food resources – although the percentage of people living in Africa since the 1990s has fallen, there are now more people in poverty because of this huge growth in population. Many African countries are still reliant on a single product for export and at the mercy of buyers from around the world. In Ethiopia, the average coffee-bean farmer lives on less than $2 a day, which cannot sustain his family. Ethiopia is one of the world's main producers of coffee beans and the country is reliant on this one product for trade with other countries. Indeed, 69 per cent of Ethiopia's exports are coffee beans and this makes up over 6 per cent of the country's GDP. Poor harvests and unfair trade agreements can hamper the economic growth of a country like Ethiopia. Although fair-trade initiatives have been introduced, unfair trade still exists and coffee and cocoa farmers often get less than 1 per cent of the price of the goods they provide. Growing these cash crops can have a devastating impact on local communities – as more good quality land is taken up growing cash crops for money, many Africans rely on imported food to eat. Up to 2000 native foodstuffs have become extinct in Africa as the diversity of what is grown is reduced.

Conflict

Africa is a very diverse continent and has a long history of conflict between different religious groups and often between governments/ dictators and civilians, in the form of civil war. This has been particularly true in the North of Africa in recent years. When conflict breaks out, it affects every aspect of people's lives; children can no longer go to school as people flee their homes, hospitals are overrun with casualties that they cannot treat, armed conflict destroys the social services that are in place and people escape to other countries and face being refugees. A lack of basic amenities such as shelter, sanitation and food means that many millions of Africans struggle to survive, let alone develop. The cost of armed conflict to Africa in the last 15 years alone has been over $300 billion.

Case study: South Sudan

South Sudan was created as a country in 2011 when it split from the rest of Sudan as the result of civil war. Since then, the country has been marred by its own civil war and failed attempts at peace deals have resulted in a humanitarian crisis. Nearly 5 million people have been displaced by conflict in the country, making it impossible for these people to access jobs and schooling or even farm the land. The UN estimates that around 55 per cent of South Sudan's population require immediate humanitarian aid due to hunger and food shortages. Although humanitarian aid has been given by several agencies, many are now reluctant to send in troops to assist as an estimated 28 aid workers were killed in the region in 2017. It is currently thought to be one of the most dangerous places in the world to live.

Figure 11.2 South Sudan

Case study: Terrorism in Africa

In addition to civil wars, many African countries are badly affected by terrorism. Areas in the North and West of Africa, in particular, face grave danger from groups such as ISIS, Boko Haram and the Islamic Maghreb. In March 2018, at least 35 people died in a series of terrorist attacks in Ouagadougou, Burkina Faso's capital city. Around 25 people were also killed in a Turkish restaurant in the capital the previous year. In total, there were an estimated 1500 terrorist attacks in Africa in 2017 alone.

Bad government and corruption

Developed countries are fortunate enough to have relatively stable governments that provide their people with the access to healthcare and education and the welfare they need. In the aftermath of colonialism and European leadership, a struggle for power and instability has emerged in many African countries. Many of these developing countries are not democratic and they face tyrannical leaders, a lack of human rights and no form of social or economic help. In the worst cases, dictators dramatically hinder development and conflict erupts from attempts to overthrow the oppressive government. Violence can break out after elections when people are forced to vote a certain way, and elections are often rigged. Members of opposition parties face violence or even death, along with their followers. Government corruption costs an estimated $60 billion in Africa every year.

Indeed, many international organisations have stated that bad government hinders development in the African continent more than any other factor, as it is the root cause of other problems such as a lack of education and healthcare facilities. With armed conflict in no fewer than four countries, seventeen countries classified as authoritarian regimes, and only ten countries considered to have democratic institutions, it is no wonder that Africa is a continent of conflict.

Case study: Somalia – corruption

According to Transparency International, Somalia ranks as the most corrupt country in the world. Although a government was formed in 2017 after years of political unrest, the election was rife with corruption with many politicians accepting bribes and buying their seats. The election was marred by violence, intimidation and lack of female representatives. The country also receives little help from the international community as it is such a dangerous place to work and live. Many journalists, aid workers and lawyers have been killed in recent years and around 500 people were killed by terrorist group Al-Shabaab in the country in 2017. All of these factors combined have led Somalia to have one of the lowest standards of living in the world due to violence, lack of economic opportunities and poor access to healthcare and education.

> ### Hints & tips ★
>
> Make sure that you can analyse the impact that lack of development has on both individuals within a country and their governments. In essays make sure you are weighing up which social, economic and political factors have the most negative impact on a country's development and why. You should also use case studies to evidence this.

Attempts to resolve a lack of development in Africa

Many developed countries around the world see it as their moral responsibility to help the African continent recover from its problems and develop. The enormous scale of Africa's social, economic and political issues does mean, however, that providing countries with aid is very difficult to manage, and it is hard to ensure that the aid is delivered to those who are most in need. There are many ethical, economic and cultural implications of providing aid assistance, which can be given in many different guises, such as bilateral or multilateral aid or through non-governmental organisations (NGOs).

We will look at possible aid solutions to resolve Africa's multitude of problems and analyse their effectiveness.

Bilateral aid

Bilateral aid is given from a donor country to a recipient country. Every year the UK gives aid assistance to African countries through the Department for International Development (DFID). Around 64 per cent of the aid money that Britain gives goes in bilateral aid to specific country projects. In 2017, two of the top five recipient countries of UK bilateral aid were in Africa – Ethiopia and Nigeria – which together received around £654 million. Many other major world powers, such as the USA, give bilateral aid to Africa. In 2017, the UK spent 0.7 per cent of its GDP on international aid. In a time of recession in Britain, however, many people are unhappy about £654 million being spent on international aid to Africa; many feel that in a time of austerity the money should be spent on welfare in the UK. The Government, though, believes it has an obligation to help developing countries around the world that do not have the same social services and facilities that are enjoyed in Britain, and many people feel that citizens in other countries are worse off than themselves.

Case study: DFID aid to the African region 2018–2019

According to DFID, aid spending on Africa for 2018–2019 focuses on these top three goals:

- funding agricultural initiatives (£38 million)
- setting up trade links in East Africa (£21 million)
- reducing the number of maternal deaths (£66 million).

DFID's main aims for Africa are to help support the continent to help itself by improving farming techniques and boosting economic trade opportunities. It also provides emergency aid in times of humanitarian crisis. DFID has dedicated a lot of funding recently to the Sahel region of Africa – an area in the north of the continent around the Sahara Desert. It has aimed to reduce food insecurity

$\Rightarrow$

in the area, which has resulted from drought, conflict, terrorism and interrupted food production. DFID wants to ensure that another 2.5 million people are food secure in the Sahel region by 2019 by providing food assistance and humanitarian aid. In East Africa, DFID is working to improve the infrastructure of many countries, which will help facilitate better trade. It aims to ensure that 3.2 million more people in the region have electricity by 2021 and promote £300 million worth of investment in agricultural deals to boost farmers' incomes. Lastly, DFID wants to reduce the number of maternal deaths and improve family planning by ensuring better access to contraceptives, preventing FGM (Female Genital Mutilation) in up to 20,000 areas and reducing the spread of Ebola.

Source: DFID

Figure 11.3 The location of the Sahel region

The effectiveness of bilateral aid

Bilateral aid is well funded and uses the resources available to whole governments. This means that the aid provided is based on a vast array of experience, experts and supplies. In the past, the UK used to give bilateral aid which was 'tied aid'. This meant that it benefited the UK as well as the African country that received it. For example, the recipient country may have had to use the UK aid money to buy British products or they may have had to allow a British military base to be built in their country in return for aid assistance. Nowadays, the UK has committed to giving bilateral aid which is never tied aid. However, there have been criticisms of bilateral aid provided by DFID in recent years; a report in 2016 found that around 25 per cent of DFID's aid budget was spent by other government departments through the cross-government Conflict, Stability and Safety Fund. This has led to questions about transparency, as it is less clear where aid money is being spent. Aid agencies have also criticised this cross-government initiative, as it has increased spending on bureaucracy, reducing the impact the money can have on recipient countries.

Multilateral aid

Multilateral aid is given from a group of countries to a recipient country. This can be through international aid agreements or international organisations such as the African Union (AU), the European Union (EU) and the United Nations (UN).

Multilateral aid and the EU

The EU gives aid to African countries through EuropeAid. The EU's current aid budget for 2014–2020 totals €30.5 billion. Around 12 per cent of this figure is spent in Africa – amounting to around €3.6 billion. The EU is the largest official donor of development assistance in the world and its main aims are to aid developing countries financially, support them in building their own infrastructure and promote human rights. EuropeAid is estimated to be behind around 25 per cent of all aid projects in Africa. The UK's involvement in EuropeAid will be up for discussion during and after Brexit negotiations.

Case study: Farmers' Africa Programme (EU multilateral aid)

Agricultural output for African countries is vital – it still provides the largest income for Africa and is essential for feeding the continent. Growing food in Africa presents many challenges. Despite some technological developments and aid to the continent, many areas still lack the equipment and education that would allow for more effective farming. The Farmers' Africa Programme aims to set up farmers' organisations – groups of farmers who can come together to share resources and expertise and who can form a union to challenge policy makers. Since the implementation of the programme in 2009, over 50 million farmers are now members of farmers' organisations in 68 different branches across Africa. The EU estimates that over 200,000 farmers received agricultural education and countries like Morocco saw a 75 per cent increase in fruit production because of the programme. Cassava farmers in Uganda who were involved in the programme saw a 210 per cent increase in profits made from selling their cassavas.

Source: European Commission

Case study: EU promotion of trade in West Africa

The EU works to provide aid programmes that promote trade in the West African region. The EU has helped farmers and producers in the West of Africa to produce goods that are in line with international safety standards. This has allowed greater trade between West African countries and the EU. This programme has trained laboratory staff, farmers and manufacturers to ensure that their produce meets international standards and has worked with over 120 businesses. The programme has also provided farming equipment and staff to train food producers and lab technicians. This has created better trade opportunities within West Africa and has seen a 280 per cent increase in exports from the region to the EU, boosting the economy of West Africa.

Source: European Commission

Multilateral aid and the United Nations

The UN gives aid to African countries through its **specialised agencies**. There are many specialised agencies, but the ones that are best known for their work in Africa are:

- FAO (Food and Agriculture Organization)
- WHO (World Health Organization)
- UNICEF (United Nations International Children's Emergency Fund).

UN Sustainable Development Goals (2015–)

In the past, we used to talk about the UN's Millennium Development Goals, which were eight development targets UN countries wanted to achieve by 2015. A huge amount of progress was made towards these goals but, after review in 2015, 17 new targets to promote international development were agreed:

- No poverty
- Zero hunger
- Good health
- Quality education
- Gender equality
- Clean water
- Clean energy
- Economic growth
- Innovation
- Reducing inequalities
- Sustainable cities
- Responsible consumption and production
- Climate action
- Cleaner seas
- Sustainable land initiatives
- Peace
- Working together through stronger partnerships

> ### Key term
>
> **Specialised agency:** The UN is split into different organisations called 'specialised agencies'. Each specialised agency has a different remit and different goals for development, for example UNESCO (United Nations Educational, Scientific and Cultural Organization) may be concerned with providing fairer education for girls.

These goals are incredibly ambitious for any country, but particularly for developing countries in Africa. Some of these goals are the same as the Millennium Development Goals but there is also now a stronger focus on gender equality and environment issues. Poorer countries are disproportionately affected by climate change. It is intended that these goals be achieved by the end of 2030, and although major progress has been made with the help of UN aid, the problems that Africa faces are often too widespread to tackle completely. It is worth noting that each individual goal will have differing degrees of success.

UNICEF in Democratic Republic of the Congo (DRC)

The United Nations International Children's Emergency Fund (UNICEF) is a UN specialised agency that works all over the world. Recent projects have focused on helping improve health in the Democratic Republic of the Congo (DRC). The agency vaccinated an estimated 3 million people in the DRC in 2017 to protect them from contracting polio. It also helped to provide emergency medical care during a recent Ebola outbreak and vaccinated 3000 people in the areas of the DRC affected to prevent the disease from spreading. The DRC has recently been affected by severe civil war, and as a result there is a hunger crisis in the area and poorer access to healthcare. UNICEF helped feed an estimated 210,000 people in the DRC during the civil war by providing emergency food aid. It also set up temporary schools allowing for 2.7 million children to access basic primary education. This type of work is vital in saving lives in small African communities but does little to fix the overall problems, like civil war, which cause these issues.

World Health Organization (WHO) in Zambia

The WHO works in 48 countries in Africa to improve the health of the African people. Its main aims are to reduce the prevalence of HIV/AIDS, malaria and polio and to provide immunisation programmes; one of its main programmes is the treatment and prevention of HIV/AIDS. In 2018, the WHO worked in Zambia to:

● promote maternal health
● improve access to sexual health information and family planning
● reduce and prevent the spread of the top six illnesses including HIV and tuberculosis (TB)
● improve healthcare for newborn babies and information on breastfeeding.

The WHO's work within Zambia has helped to improve the healthcare situation in many areas. Maternal health has improved, with fewer deaths in childbirth and mothers receiving better health information on nutrition and breastfeeding. Zambia has made progress towards the 90-90-90 HIV targets with a rate of 67-87-89. This means that 67 per cent of people who are HIV positive are now aware of their status (thanks to HIV screening programmes offered by the WHO). There has also been increased access to antiretroviral medications in Zambia to treat HIV. Lastly, Zambia now has polio-free status, meaning that polio is no longer a health concern in the country thanks to immunisation programmes which have been offered by organisations like the WHO. These organisations have been very successful in improving healthcare outcomes on a local level within African countries and have saved the lives of millions of Africans. They are restricted in what they can achieve, however, by bigger issues such as a country's government, policies, infrastructure, funding and conditions like civil war and famine.

The effectiveness of multilateral aid

By far the largest benefit of multilateral aid, compared to other types of aid, is how well funded it is: the combined funding of several groups of countries means that larger, more effective projects can be undertaken that are likely to reach more people and be better resourced. This type of aid is also argued to be more reliable than other types: donor countries feel safer donating to a project involving several countries, where the economic burden can be shared. Countries are also more likely to achieve more by working together. However, the work of multilateral organisations can be minimal in countries that are not democracies as giving to these countries does not ensure that resources or money go to the people in most need. Also, bad government, violence and civil war within some African countries all limit what agencies can do. There can also be other problems, for example, according to the UN Department for Safety and Security, the UN pulled troops out of the southern region of Malawi in 2017 after violent gangs attacked civilians and aid workers who they accused of vampirism! This is a key example of how local beliefs of witchcraft in rural African villages can interfere with aid work.

Non-Governmental Organisations (NGOs)

NGOs provide aid to developing countries through charitable donations. Some of the most famous NGOs include Save the Children, Oxfam, Christian Aid, the Red Cross and the Bill & Melinda Gates Foundation. These organisations work on a variety of different levels, often on regional or local projects within different countries, and on a smaller scale than multilateral aid. Relying on charitable funding reduces the funds available to NGOs, but the advantage is that they can set their own aid agendas and are not influenced by governments.

Case study: Oxfam in Ethiopia

Oxfam works in nearly every African country. In Ethiopia, recent projects have involved improving gender inequality and reducing violence against women (in line with Sustainable Development Goal 5 – gender equality). The projects have helped many female farmers improve their farming techniques, crop yields and access to financial services. In some areas, the programme has helped improve farmers' revenues by 11 per cent and access to clean water has reduced women's daily workloads by up to seven hours as they no longer have to walk for miles to collect water. Also, vaccination of livestock has meant healthier animals that can be used for both farming and

Figure 11.4 Oxfam logo

consumption. A recent women's empowerment initiative has tried to promote female equality – this has helped to change marriage culture so that no girl under 18 can marry. This has helped prevent an estimated 500 child marriages so far and helped to reduce gender violence by providing support groups for women.

Case study: Bill & Melinda Gates Foundation

Bill Gates, the founder of Microsoft, and his wife Melinda have established an extremely successful NGO called the Bill & Melinda Gates Foundation. Billionaires Bill and Melinda Gates, along with other donors such as Warren Buffett, have been praised for their philanthropy work. The foundation has pledged to invest $5 billion in aid projects from 2016 to 2021 across ten African countries. This money is to help fund immunisation projects and provide livestock. Their project to reduce infant mortality rates (IMRs) in Rwanda has seen a 30 per cent drop in IMRs since 2008 due to the promotion of breastfeeding, skin-to-skin contact and better maternal medical education. The foundation is also believed to be behind vaccination projects in seven African countries, which have eradicated trachoma – a leading cause of blindness. According to *The Guardian*, the work funded by the foundation has saved an estimated 122 million lives worldwide since 1990. Although NGOs are often limited in what they can achieve, because they rely on charitable donations, the Bill & Melinda Gates Foundation is an excellent example of how NGOs can make a massive impact globally.

The effectiveness of NGOs

NGOs undeniably provide essential life-saving humanitarian aid to many millions of people in African countries. Their work impacts on communities by improving access to education, healthcare and safe drinking water, and is vital during times of international emergency. The role that NGOs play in Africa is ever increasing; for example, the number of registered NGOs working in Kenya has increased four-fold in the last ten years.

The work of NGOs has been criticised for many reasons, however. Firstly, many people have argued that they provide temporary fixes to humanitarian problems but do little to address the causes of these issues. Also, they usually work on a smaller scale than multilateral and bilateral approaches and many small NGOs can be working on the same issues in the same areas rather than taking on larger and more successful projects. Some NGOs have been criticised for bringing in their own staff to deal with issues rather than empowering local Africans to be part of the solution to the problem. Nowadays NGOs are under more intense scrutiny from the public who want to know exactly where their donations are going. This has called for greater transparency as to where NGOs spend money and has led to criticisms of the way in which NGOs are financed as a lot of money donated to them is spent on bureaucracy and administration rather than going directly to the people in need. Some NGOs have recently been hit by a number of high-profile scandals, which can affect the NGOs' credibility and reduce the amount of money they receive in donations. For example, in 2018 Oxfam staff were accused of hiring sex workers while working to provide aid in Haiti. It is thought that this type of scandal will impact on the amount of charitable donations that the NGO receives.

Hints & tips ★

In essays, it is not enough to simply describe the ways in which NGOs, countries and alliances provide aid. You need to analyse the impact that these organisations have on Africa's development and analyse both the advantages and drawbacks of these types of aid in promoting development. Make sure you evidence your line of argument with learned case studies.

Part Five: Assignment and essay writing

Chapter 12
Unlocking the assignment marks

Chapter 2 provides a summary of the requirements of the assignment. Now we will take you through each stage of your research and written report. As you are aware, marks are allocated to different parts of your report.

Table 12.1 Allocation of marks

1A	Identifying and demonstrating knowledge and understanding of the issue about which a decision is to be made including alternative course(s) of action	**10 marks**
1B	Analysing and synthesising information from a range of sources including use of specified resources	**10 marks**
1C	Evaluating the usefulness and reliability of a range of sources of information	**2 marks**
1D	Communicating information using the convention of a report	**4 marks**
1E	Reaching a decision supported by evidence about the issues	**4 marks**

Choosing your Modern Studies issue

It is crucial that you choose a relevant and appropriate topic. You should choose a Modern Studies issue that interests you. It can be a political, social or international issue.

Issues along the lines of *Should wolves be re-introduced to Scotland?* or *Should Britain introduce voluntary euthanasia?* are not Modern Studies issues and should not be chosen.

Your teacher will give you advice, and you should listen and be prepared to change your topic if they say your preferred issue is not a contemporary Modern Studies issue.

Your assignment is a report and not an essay. A title such as *The President of the USA is too powerful* should be avoided. It could easily be an essay if you add the word *Discuss*. It would be very difficult to turn this into a decision-making report and the temptation would be to write an essay.

Hints & tips

Be careful that your issue is a Modern Studies issue and not one more relevant to Religious, Moral and Philosophic Studies (RMPS) or environmental science.

Remember

If your title is not appropriate you will immediately lose 4 of the 10 marks available for the knowledge section of your report.

Structuring your report

There is no one model to use in developing your title. Two different report models are recommended.

Model one

This is a straightforward decision-making report as outlined below:

Should free prescriptions for all be introduced in England?

As stated, the possible disadvantage of adopting a straightforward decision-making report is that if you do not consider a possible third option you will be penalised 1 mark in the analysing information section, so you will only be able to receive a maximum 9 out of 10 marks. Refer to the example on page 139 whereby the candidate's section *Reaching a decision* becomes a third option.

Remember

If you only consider two options, you can only receive a maximum of 9 marks out of 10 for the analysis section.

Model two

This involves building a report around a broad issue with three options as outlined below:
The broad issue chosen is *child poverty* and the three options are:

1 Introduce free school meals for all
2 Introduce longer nursery hours
3 End the freeze on Child Benefit payments.

Marker's comment

All three options clearly link to the issue of child poverty and provide opportunities for the student to display relevant and up-to-date knowledge of the issue. It also provides an opportunity to perhaps research the welfare reforms of the UK coalition Government and any actions taken by the Scottish Government such as the introduction of free school meals for primary 1–3. So, this is an excellent range of options.

One drawback of model two is the amount of research you will have to undertake in what is basically three decision-making exercises.
The model two approach clearly considers three options and would therefore be able to access the full 30 marks. If you decide to adopt the broad issue approach then you must be careful that your three options are relevant to the issue as outlined above. Below is an example of a poorly constructed title:
The broad issue chosen is *unemployment in the UK*, and the three options are:

1 Raise the minimum wage
2 Increase tax credits
3 End zero-hour contracts.

Marker's comment

The issue is too general and too vague. The options chosen are more to do with reducing poverty than with unemployment. Employers might argue that ending zero-hour contracts would create greater unemployment. Increasing tax credits does not have a direct link. So, this is a poor range of options.

Below is an example of excellent practice in offering a three-style option.

The broad issue chosen is *reducing poverty in the UK*, and the three options are:

1 Raise the Government Living Wage/National Minimum Wage
2 Restore tax credits to their previous value
3 End the freeze to Child Benefit and all welfare payments.

Marker's comment

The issue is completely up to date and centres round the significant cuts to welfare payments since the Conservatives came to power in 2010. It covers both the working poor and the unemployed and the debate around collectivism and individualism.

1A Identifying and demonstrating knowledge and understanding

Framing your issue – the introduction

Both models will need a detailed introduction that outlines your chosen issue and the reasons why you have chosen that issue. You could also introduce and discuss, in this section, what your option choices are. This introduction section is where you can unlock, access and secure the first 5 knowledge marks that are awarded for framing your issue and setting the scene for your investigation.

The introduction gives you the opportunity to impress the examiner with your background knowledge and awareness of your chosen issue.

The more relevant and detailed knowledge you present, the more marks you will pick up. So, spending a little time on this section will be worthwhile and will have you well on the way to an A grade.

You could include the following:

- several detailed and properly exemplified paragraphs that show knowledge and understanding of the key points/areas of the issue you have chosen
- some discussion and explanation of why you think this is an important issue – you could also include what governments or organisations have done regarding your issue or what impact your issue has had on society
- an introduction to and discussion about your option choices before you go on to investigate each option in further detail later on in your report.

Below is a sample introduction paragraph on the issue of child poverty.

Sample marked paragraph

Child poverty is an issue that affects many children and families in the UK. It is, for some, a growing issue that has led to different governments in both Scotland and the rest of the UK introducing different policies to try to tackle it. By investigating and researching this issue, I aim to come up with a recommendation that effectively tackles and reduces child poverty by introducing either Free School Meals, increasing the Minimum Wage for lone parents or by increasing Child Benefits.

Some people believe that the Government has a role to collectively provide for its citizens through the ideas of the Welfare State. Others, however, believe that the individual is responsible in looking after themselves. (BK) The Collectivists believe that recent Coalition policies such as the Bedroom Tax and the cap on benefits has increased the number of children in poverty. Child poverty can lead to poorer health, a poorer education and can affect someone's life chances such as job opportunities and earnings in later life. (BK)

Child poverty can be caused by a number of things – unemployment, government policies and family type. Child poverty can rise as well as fall with government policy being important in affecting this. For example, child poverty fell in the first decade of this century when government policies were more effective at tackling child poverty. (BK)

Marker's comment

Candidate displays excellent knowledge. The issue is framed well with mention of founding principles of Welfare State, collectivism and individualism, some knowledge of the impact of coalition policies (Bedroom Tax, etc.), impact of child poverty on education and health, factors causing child poverty. Overall, it is a good strong section.

Perhaps needs a bit more specific detail and statistics to back up some of the points made, but the candidate is well on the way to unlocking the 5 marks for framing the issue. Candidate correctly labelled anything they thought was background/framing knowledge by using (BK).

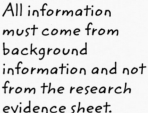

Remember

All information must come from background information and not from the research evidence sheet.

Knowledge used to support analysis

To access the other 5 knowledge marks available, the candidate needs to provide knowledge in support of any decision or recommendation that is made as part of the research findings. This knowledge is used in support of the candidate's research evidence but should not be written on their research evidence sheet as this would make any knowledge evidence presented by the candidate invalid as it would no longer be knowledge.

Remember

The 5 marks are dependent upon the:

☞ quality of background information
☞ level of detail given
☞ range of information used to support different aspects of the analysis
☞ synthesis of background information with research evidence.

An effective method of approaching these knowledge marks is to introduce a piece of relevant background knowledge every time you use information from your research evidence sheet in support of a decision or recommendation. For example:

> *One reason why I have decided to recommend extending the smoking ban to all public parks and open public spaces is that it has worked in cutting poor health in other places where it has been introduced. Source 1 backs this up as it shows that in Western Australia, where the ban is in place, smoking rates have decreased and life expectancy has increased. This proves that the policy has worked and should be introduced in Scotland. From my own background knowledge, I know that in New York this policy has been in operation since 2011 and has had an impact on the number of smokers giving up. Since 2011, there has been a 7% fall in the number of smokers. (BK) The source information and my background information show that the policy is having a positive impact where it has already been introduced and would have a similar positive impact here and should be considered as an option in improving health.*

Marker's comment

Candidate makes a recommendation for a particular decision and justifies their decision by synthesising source information with their own relevant background information. The candidate has identified where they have used their own background knowledge by using 'BK' in brackets and the phrase, 'from my own background knowledge'.

1B Analysing and synthesising information from a range of resources including specified resources

The most important thing for you to remember is that it is what you do with your evidence on the research evidence sheet that will dictate how many marks you will receive for the 'analysing and synthesising information' section.

Using your research evidence sheet

You must use the evidence appropriately to support your explanation, analysis and evaluation of the issue, and any decisions or recommendations should flow from the findings of your investigation/assignment.

Using the research evidence sheet effectively and correctly is key to unlocking and achieving the full range of the **10 marks** available. You can include primary/secondary research and statistical, graphical or numerical data. You can also include survey results, quotations, interview questions and responses, newspaper articles, information from textbooks, webpage data and screen shots.

To sum up:

Your research evidence sheet is *not* a:
- detailed plan of your write-up
- paragraph-by-paragraph structure prompt sheet
- sheet that you lift and simply copy
- sheet that simply lists a range of website addresses with no reference to their content.

Therefore you must avoid:
- copying information from your research evidence sheet in isolation with no analysis or development
- writing too little on your research evidence sheet that means that analysis and synthesis marks cannot be awarded, for example writing simply 'www.theguardian.com'
- using the research evidence sheet like a structured report plan with headings and prompts
- not making reference to your research evidence sheet during the write-up stage.

Further good practice:
- Label your sources, for example, Source A, Source B, and refer to these specifically in your write-up, for example: *Source A states that … this is backed up by Source B's statistics which show …*
- Use the 'less is more' approach to the research evidence sheet. In other words, a brief description of what the source is that you are using on your research evidence sheet, for example, *Source A is a BBC article from their website (URL …) that looks at the arguments both for and against an extension of the smoking ban.* Your reference source might contain some statistics about the decline in the number of smokers as well as a quote from the Chief Medical Officer.

Once you have assessed all the evidence and made a recommendation/decision regarding a specific course of action, you will need to justify your decision based upon research evidence and your own background knowledge of the issue.

To achieve a high mark for this section, you should look to give detailed analysis of the source evidence that supports your decision as well as synthesising your source material either from within or between the sources that you have used.

> **Hints & tips** ⭐
>
> *You can include relevant facts and different viewpoints, for example a quotation from a pressure group or politician. It is what you do with the evidence that is crucial. The more analysis, evaluation and explanation you use, combined with the synthesis of your various strands of evidence, the more likely you are to achieve 10 marks for this section.*

> **Remember**
>
> Do something with your information:
> ☞ Explain
> ☞ Evaluate
> ☞ Analyse
> ☞ Synthesise.

Introducing a piece of background information to further reinforce or back up your decision also gives you the opportunity to access some of the 'Knowledge in support of analysis' marks that are available.

Analysing and synthesising sample paragraph

One reason in favour of my recommendation that Scotland should become an independent country is that it would be more democratic as Scotland often ends up with governments it never voted for. Democracy should mean that the people's views are heard and represented. Source B, which is an article from the 'National' newspaper supports this analysis as it states that 'Decisions taken by government are best made when they are made by people who live there. Westminster doesn't reflect the political mood in Scotland'. Evidence from Source A also reinforces this point with the information that only 1 of Scotland's 59 MPs is from the ruling Conservative Party. Clearly a more representative system of government is needed for Scotland if the views of its people are to be heard. Indeed, as Source B correctly states, this would be a 'democratic deficit' for the Scottish people and it is something that needs to change. This shows that only by becoming an independent nation can Scotland get rid of this 'democratic deficit', which is why I have made this recommendation.

Marker's comment

Decision stated and evidence presented in support of the decision. Evidence of synthesis from within and between sources as well as reference to specific research source material. Reference to political aspect of issue in terms of representation as well as explanation and analysis. Overall 3 marks awarded.

> **Remember**
>
> If you do not make reference to the research evidence, the most marks you can achieve for this section is 5.

1C Evaluating the usefulness and reliability of a range of sources of information

This section is worth **2 marks** and you shouldn't spend too long unlocking these marks. Getting this section out of the way quickly and effectively is important.

You need to assess/evaluate the usefulness of the sources used on your resource sheet. Areas such as objectivity and bias, nature of a source, reliability and trustworthiness, etc. should be referred to in the answer.

You can comment on individual sources or compare two sources. One approach that can be effective is to compare two sources, preferably the most reliable and least reliable of the sources used. This will allow for greater comparison and contrast. For example, comparison between an outdated adapted source from a biased pressure group and a recent

> **Remember**
>
> The sources assessed must be from the resource sheet. If you evaluate a source not on the sheet, no marks will be awarded, regardless of the quality of the response.

set of statistics from a respected opinion poll organisation or the Office of National Statistics would provide sufficient opportunity for you to achieve the 2 marks, as the example below shows:

My most reliable source came from a textbook 'The Politics of Electoral College Reform' (Source 3). It is a book that provides many different opinions and arguments on this issue that are all relevant today. It is written by respected academics from Yale University and subject to academic rigour. My least reliable source was an opinion poll from Gallup News (Source 5), which is a respected independent organisation. However, the survey sample covers only 1000 US citizens and as such it is difficult to conclude that it accurately represents the views of a population the size of America.

Marker's comment

Candidate achieves both marks for this section as they have commented effectively and appropriately on the usefulness of their source material as referenced on the research evidence sheet.

1D Communicating information using the convention of a report

As indicated, there are many ways to structure your report/investigation, but the two most common and effective ways of approaching it are:

- Make your decision early on in the report and then justify your decision by using your research evidence and own background knowledge in support of it after your decision
- Discuss your various options, giving evidence from your research evidence sheet and own background knowledge and then come to, and justify, your decision at the end of your report.

SQA 'convention of a report' criteria

- Structure – including the use of headings and sections where appropriate to organise information
- Report style – including the use of appropriate social science terminology
- Reference to evidence used – including research evidence and background knowledge of issue
- Consistency, coherence and logic of argument

1E Reaching a decision

You can score a maximum of **4 marks** for reaching a decision supported by evidence about the issue.

The marks are allocated in terms of:

- clarity of decision reached and quality of evidence used to support decision
- explanation for rejection of alternative decisions/courses of action.

The justification for your decision should be running through the main body of the report write-up, providing evidence for your course of action as well as an acknowledgement of why you didn't go for the other option(s).

A 2-mark response would give a decision supported by detailed evidence. The bar is set a bit higher for the full 4 marks as the decision would have to be supported by detailed evidence and evaluation as to why the decision is preferred to alternative(s).

Commenting on and including reasons why you rejected the other options gives you a greater opportunity of accessing the 4 marks, depending upon the level of detailed evidence provided. You should also consider evaluating which argument or evidence is the strongest or most convincing.

The conclusion should also be considered for re-stating the main reasons for recommendation while recognising reasons against the alternative options.

Below is a Model A approach with the straightforward title *Should free prescriptions for all be introduced in England?* The candidate below also unlocks the missing mark by considering a third option.

Sample decision/recommendation/conclusion paragraph

Reaching a decision

While I am persuaded by the arguments for the introduction of free prescriptions for all, I am aware that further massive cuts will be made to public expenditure in the period 2015–2020 and that it might be difficult to introduce this policy. However, I do not wish simply to recommend retention of charges, as I accept the above financial arguments. As such I have decided to propose a third option as the first step in gradually introducing free prescriptions as outlined in the conclusion below.

Option 3: Free prescriptions in England for all those with long-term illnesses

As I have argued, I do not accept the viewpoint that free prescriptions are a waste of money, rather it is value for money. I have been impressed by the evidence presented by the Prescription Charge Coalition and it is most unfair that two
individuals with serious health conditions in the UK depend on the lottery of location. Emily Watt, an English student from Liverpool and one of those interviewed by the Coalition states: 'it is a tax on ill health for the English public and its basically prescription apartheid.' **(Research evidence 4)** *She was diagnosed in 2010 at the age of 18 with ulcerative colitis and will need to take medicine for the rest of her life. I support the collective viewpoint and would hope that in future years free prescriptions can gradually be implemented with students as the next category to be exempted from charges.*

Marker's comment

This is an excellent way to unlock the missing mark by considering a third option. Here the candidate recognises the justice of free prescriptions for all but takes into consideration the economic argument against.

Chapter 13
Unlocking the essay marks

Parts Two to Four of this book have focused on the course content for each of the individual study themes. This is the material and information that you will have to know in order to achieve a very good pass in the subject. Without learning this information, you will not be able to maximise your marks and get the pass that you deserve.

This section will now take the information from the previous chapters and show you how to put it together and to construct really good and effective essay responses to the questions that could be asked in the final exam.

This section will take the fear out of the exam and prepare you, with all the tools and technical knowledge of structure and content to help you, to unlock as many marks as you possibly can. By knowing how to structure your responses and how to answer the essay questions effectively and correctly, you will be increasing your opportunities for achieving a really good 'A' pass in the subject.

The most important thing to remember when sitting Higher Modern Studies is that you will give yourself the best opportunity for maximising your marks by attempting to answer **the question asked**. This seems rather obvious and common sense, but many, many students fall into the trap of telling the examiner everything they know about an area rather than tailoring their essay response to answer the question fully.

For example, if the question asks you to 'Evaluate the importance of social class on voting behaviour', you need to discuss how important it is in affecting how people vote in elections, how its influence may have changed and how important it is in influencing other factors. Your focus should be on social class, its importance and how it affects other factors. Some students will make the mistake of seeing the words 'voting behaviour' in the question and then proceed to tell you everything they know about all of the various factors involved in influencing voting behaviour. This usually takes the form of a collection of unlinked and unrelated paragraphs that mention a variety of factors with little mention of the main focus of the question, which in this case is the importance of social class on voting behaviour.

A candidate who uses this 'Let's throw everything at the question and hope that some of the information gets credit' strategy will struggle to achieve more than a third of the overall marks for the question. So, always attempt to answer the specific question asked of you. By doing this you will maximise the marks available for the question and make it easy for the examiner or marker to use the full range of marks available when marking your essay.

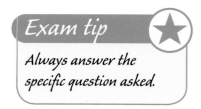

Exam tip

Always answer the specific question asked.

The exam

As stated, in Higher Modern Studies there are three parts to your assessment:

- the assignment
- question paper 1 (the essays)
- question paper 2 (the enquiry skills questions).

See Chapter 12 for more information on the assignment, and how to use the assignment to boost your overall mark and improve your chances of an excellent pass grade in the subject. In the assignment, you have the freedom to choose your area of study and the resources and sources used. It is worthwhile choosing an area for your dissertation that you genuinely enjoy and have a keen interest in. For the assignment, knowing the background to the issue and using your sources appropriately and effectively to support or reject your decisions or options will boost your marks and mean that you can approach the two question papers with assurance and confidence.

For question paper 1, you will need to answer three essays in total, with a question coming from each of the three sections (Political, Social and International Issues).

The total number of marks available is 52, with two essays worth **20 marks** and one essay worth **12 marks**.

You have 1 hour 45 minutes to respond to these questions. This is not a lot of time, so time management is absolutely vital, and you should practise your essay timings. Aim to not spend too much time on one question as this means that there won't be enough time to answer the other two questions fully. You should always aim to finish three questions. Only doing two or two and a bit of the essays will cost you marks and will affect your overall grade. A good time management trick is to work out beforehand how long you should spend on each essay.

The location of the 12-mark question can change from exam to exam, moving between the three sections. The best way to prepare for this is to plan your study and revision around answering 20-mark questions and reduce the length of answer and content for your 12-mark responses. It is easier to plan for all 20-mark responses and remove some of the points than it is to plan for 12-mark responses and then try to add points during an exam. Doing this should diminish some of the fear and panic that students often face when trying to tackle 12- and 20-mark responses.

You will have the choice of two questions in both the Social Issues and International Issues sections and the choice of three questions in the Democracy in Scotland and the UK section.

> ### Exam tip ★
>
> *Effective time management is essential. You should spend no more than 40 minutes on a 20-mark essay and no more than 25 minutes on a 12-mark essay. Once you have reached the allotted time, move on to the next essay.*

Types of questions

The types of questions that can be asked in question paper 1 come from the SQA Course Assessment Specification (CAS) and are limited to the following areas for each of the specific study themes.

For Democracy in Scotland and the UK, the questions asked can be from the following areas:

- Possible alternatives for the governance of Scotland ☐
- Implications of the UK's decision to leave the European Union (EU) ☐
- Effectiveness of parliamentary representatives in holding government to account ☐
- Strengths and weaknesses of different electoral systems used in elections within the UK ☐
- Factors that influence voting behaviour including class, age and media ☐
- Ways in which citizens can influence government decision-making, including pressure groups ☐

Remember, three questions can be asked from these areas. This area of study is compulsory for all students.

For Social Issues in the UK, you will study either Social Inequality or Crime and the Law.

For Social Inequality, the questions asked can be from the following areas:

- Reasons why income/wealth inequality exists ☐
- Reasons why health inequalities exist ☐
- Effect of inequality on a group or groups in society ☐
- Individualist/collectivist debate ☐
- Effectiveness of measures taken to tackle inequalities, including government measures ☐

Two questions can be asked from these areas.

For Crime and the Law, the questions asked can be from the following areas:

- Legal rights and responsibilities of UK citizens ☐
- Causes and theories of crime ☐
- Impact of crime on victims, offenders and their families ☐
- Social and economic impact of crime on wider society ☐
- Effectiveness of custodial and non-custodial responses to crime ☐

Two questions can be asked from these areas.

In the International Issues section, candidates will study either World Powers or World Issues.

For World Powers, the questions asked can be from the following areas:

- Extent to which the political system allows democratic participation ☐
- Political institutions and their ability to dominate government decision-making ☐
- Socio-economic inequality and its impact on a specific group in society ☐
- Effectiveness of government responses to socio-economic inequality ☐
- A world power's international influence ☐

Two questions can be asked from these areas.

For World Issues, the questions asked can be from the following areas:

- Social, economic and political factors that have caused the issue ☐
- Effects of the issue on individuals, families and communities ☐
- Effects of the issue on the governments involved and the wider international community ☐
- Effectiveness of individual countries in tackling the issue ☐
- Effectiveness of international organisations in tackling the issue ☐

Two questions can be asked from these areas.

To help you with your revision and study, tick off the areas once you have covered them and feel confident about your ability to answer a 20-mark question on each of the specific study areas.

The question stems

In National 5, there were two different types of knowledge questions you could be asked. One was, 'Describe in detail' and the other was 'Explain in detail'. These tended to require the candidate to answer 'how' or 'why' in response to a question. For example, 'Describe in detail the powers of the first minister' or 'Explain in detail why some people prefer the FPTP voting system'. In Higher Modern Studies, the questions are slightly more technical and require a wider variety of response.

In Higher Modern Studies, you will be asked four different types of questions, each with a different question stem. The stem determines the type of response or answer you will give. Some question stems require you to analyse a particular topic, factor or area whereas other stems may require you to evaluate or weigh up how effective, influential or important something is. Or, you may be asked to discuss all the different viewpoints and opinions related to one of the topic areas you have studied.

The question stems are different for the 12- and 20-mark essay questions.

The 12-mark questions will begin with either 'Analyse' or 'Evaluate'. For example:
- Analyse the potential impact of Britain leaving the EU.
- Evaluate the importance of social class on voting behaviour.

What is the difference between these stems and how does that impact on the type of answer you give? According to the SQA, the differences between the stems are as follows:

- **Analyse** questions: Candidates gain marks for identifying parts of an issue, the relationship between these parts and their relationships with the whole; and for drawing out and relating implications.
- **Evaluate** questions: Candidates gain marks for making a judgement based on criteria; for determining the value of something.

If you think about the analyse and evaluate stems in real-life situations, it should help you get a clearer picture of what each of the stems requires from you. For example:

- Analyse the reasons why more young people prefer a beach holiday to a cruise.
- Evaluate the impact of smart phones on a young person's social life.

Using real-life examples helps us to see exactly how each question is different and requires the candidate to structure and approach each question differently. By knowing what is expected of you for each question and answering the stem prompt and question correctly, you should be able to unlock the full potential of marks.

The 20-mark questions will either begin with 'To what extent' or will take the form 'Statement – Discuss'. For example:

- To what extent have organisations been effective in tackling the issue that you have studied.
- 'The media is the most important factor in influencing the outcomes of elections'. Discuss.

Again, the SQA outline the difference:

- **To what extent** questions: Candidates gain marks for analysing the issue in the question and coming to a conclusion or conclusions which involve an evaluative judgement, which is likely to be quantitative in nature.
- **Discuss** questions: Candidates communicate ideas and information on the issue in the statement. Candidates gain marks for analysing and evaluating different views of the statement or viewpoint.

Again, by using real-life examples of these questions, it becomes clearer what the difference is and how you should structure your response to each question stem. For example:

- To what extent does having a large garden help sell your house?
- 'Love Island is more entertaining than I'm a Celebrity.' Discuss.

The 'To what extent' real-life example can generate a number of varied responses. Having a large garden could be a deal clincher if you have a young family and want somewhere safe for them to play away from traffic and other dangers. Having a large garden is not desirable for everyone though. If you are a young, busy professional who is working 10/12 hours a day then the thought of having to tend and look after a large garden will not be the deal clincher that it was for others with different needs and wants.

Allocation of marks

For 12-mark questions, up to 8 marks can be awarded for knowledge and understanding (description, explanation and exemplification). The other 4 marks are awarded for the higher order skills of analysis or evaluation. If your analysis or evaluation is very good, however, then the marks allocated for this can be increased beyond the 4 marks.

For the 20-mark questions, up to 8 marks can be awarded for knowledge and understanding (description, explanation and exemplification). The remaining 12 marks are split between the higher order skills of analysis and evaluation and structured argument with 6 marks for analysis and evaluation, 2 marks for an essay structure that follows a coherent line of argument and the final 4 marks for making judgements and drawing relevant conclusions. As with the 12-mark question, if your analysis or evaluation is very good you can be awarded more than the 6 marks.

The fully worked out examples for each of the four essay questions below show you how to tackle the essay questions and to maximise the marks available.

Questions and model answers

To what extent

Section 1: Democracy in Scotland and the United Kingdom

Question ?

To what extent does the electoral system you have studied provide fair representation?

You should refer to Scotland or the United Kingdom or both in your answer. **20 marks**

Responses will be credited that make reference to:

- the main features of the electoral system(s)
- analysis/evaluation of the ways the electoral system provides fair representation
- balanced overall evaluative comment on the extent to which the system(s) provides fair representation
- a clear, coherent line of argument.

Model answer

One electoral system I have studied is the Additional Members System. This is used in the Scottish Parliament elections. It is a hybrid voting system that is designed to include the best features of First Past The Post and the proportional element of PR systems. Under AMS, voters get two votes – one for electing a Constituency MSP and the other for electing 7 regional MSPs. This is meant to ensure that the overall result is roughly proportionate and that voters and political parties are fairly represented in Parliament. This seems to be the case as, for example, in the 2016 Scottish Parliament elections, the Conservatives received 21% of the vote and they won roughly the same percentage of seats, which can be seen to be providing fair representation.

AMS therefore allows for the views of the electorate to be represented because the number of seats a party wins is close to the proportion of votes that they have won, which means that the makeup of Parliament reflects how the public actually voted and who they voted for.

Due to the proportionate nature of AMS, it allows smaller parties a greater chance of seeing some of their candidates elected, which means it is much fairer than a system such as First Past The Post which tends to only reward those larger parties who have a greater chance of coming first in Constituencies. Although smaller parties are unlikely to come first in the Constituency vote under AMS, they still stand a very good chance of gaining one or more of the regional or list seats. Under FPTP, voters of smaller parties such as the Green Party may not turn out to vote as they know their candidate stands very little chance of success. This is not the case under AMS. Every vote counts under AMS and the Greens have had a great deal of success in the Scottish Parliament under AMS where they have won seats in every election and have even won as many as 7 seats in Scottish Parliament elections.

This means that AMS allows the views of the electorate to be represented because people feel they can really vote according to their views and that every vote is a positive vote for someone rather than a tactical vote to stop a candidate being elected. Small parties have a greater chance of being elected, which then means a broader range of views being represented in Parliament.

AMS also makes it difficult for one party to gain a majority in Parliament and it is much more likely to result in a coalition or minority government, which means that more parties need to be involved in the decision-making process and therefore ensuring that a wider variety of views are heard and wider representation. Since the creation of the Scottish Parliament in 1999, there have been coalitions, minority governments and a majority SNP government. Coalitions and minority governments means that parties have to work together and negotiate and compromise in order for laws to be passed so the views of the wider electorate are heard and the laws passed become more consensual and representative of the wider population. This shows that AMS allows for the views of the electorate to be heard rather than the supporters of just one party dictating what legislation is passed.

However, an increased chance of coalition can be seen to limit representation to some extent. When coalitions occur, the public are not asked or consulted about it and are not given an option to accept or reject this. This can be seen also as acting against the interests of the population and leads to poor representation as no one voted for or was given the option to vote for a coalition. This could be seen as being undemocratic. Supporters of one party may feel aggrieved and angry about their party working with another party as well as not agreeing with the compromises that may be made in government. This can then mean that the electorate's views are not being represented because they do not get the opportunity to vote for coalitions.

Another criticism of AMS is that it can create too many representatives and can leave voters confused about who they contact if they have an issue that needs to be resolved. It creates a two-tier system of representatives, with the constituency MSP seeing themselves as being ⇨

more senior than the 7 list MSPs. This might create a weak link between list MSPs and their voters which could lead to poor representation.

Overall, AMS can be seen to deliver fair representation as it is proportional and allows for smaller parties to get a voice in Parliament and to represent those voters of smaller parties. It also leads to coalition government, which can often mean a wider variety of views and opinions being heard as well as fairer laws being passed.

Marker's comments

A very strong answer that shows clear understanding of how AMS works and its impact on representation. Great understanding of the impact of the system on smaller parties and the fact that it allows for a more consensual type of politics. Good use of balance in the answer as well as relevant and contemporary exemplification. A really good response with a coherent line of argument. Full marks.

Discuss
Section 3, Option 2: World Issues

Question

To what extent has a world issue you have studied been resolved by international organisations? **20 marks**

Responses will be credited that make reference to:

- the responses of international organisations to development issues in Africa
- evaluation analysis of the ways international organisations attempt to resolve development issues in Africa
- balanced overall evaluative comment on the extent to which responses made by international organisations have been successful in resolving development issues in Africa
- a clear, coherent line of argument.

Up to **8 marks** for knowledge (description, explanation and exemplification) and up to **12 marks** for evaluation, analysis and structured answers.

Model answer

Development on the African continent is a very important world issue. Lack of development in African countries is a long standing issue caused by social, economic and political problems. However, many international organisations such as the UN have tried to resolve issues in African countries through aid projects and UN peacekeepers which have had varying levels of success.

The UN has aimed to have universal primary education in Africa by 2015 as part of the Millennium Development Goals. One UN agency in particular, UNICEF, has been involved in improving this. Lack of education is a massive factor that

hinders development in Africa, as education is often the best way to lift children out of poverty and improve their futures. In 2014, UNICEF continued to roll out its 'Schools for Africa' campaign, which aimed to raise a further $80 million to put towards education in thirteen African countries. This has been successful to a large extent as primary school enrolment has risen in these thirteen countries and there have been successful life skills programmes rolled out to raise awareness of HIV/AIDS. This has given more children a chance to improve their job opportunities in the future and help them try to escape poverty. However, despite all the work *carried out by UNICEF, there is still a lot of countries such as Somalia which have very poor education systems. In Somalia the enrolment rate is only 23%. UNICEF has had a fair amount of success in helping Africa develop in terms of education but there is still a massive amount of progress to be made.*

The WFP is another UN agency that has aimed to resolve lack of development in Africa by tackling hunger. Hunger is a massive problem in Africa due to high rates of poverty and lack of effective farming methods. The WFP launched their 'Food Voucher Programme' in 2012 in Somalia, which went on to help over 15,000 people. This gave families up to $80 of vouchers a month to buy food from local markets which in turn reduced hunger and boosted the local economy. Despite this success on a small scale, the hunger problem in Africa is still too big for international organisations to overcome, with over 30 million starving people in Africa. Political and social problems in African countries also hinder attempts at resolving poverty and hunger. In Somalia in 2011, the WFP also sent large food donations which were stolen and sold on the black market. This shows that WFP have not had great success in promoting development, as hunger is such a massive obstacle to overcome and often conflict within African countries can hinder effective aid from being delivered.

At present a civil war is raging in the new state of South Sudan. In 2013 the President Salva Kiir sacked the vice-president Riek Machar and ethnic conflict and armed conflict broke out. Prior to its independence in 2011 abundant international aid and access to oil revenue suggested that South Sudan would be a prosperous country. However the leaders of the new government used much of this money to expand the army and to enrich themselves. So the financial support of

international organisations has not been used to benefit the people and this highlights the limitation of international organisation's support.

The UN has sent 10,000 peacekeepers to South Sudan and the international community is trying to broker a peace deal to end the civil war. The UN Security Council is considering an arms ban on the warring factions. More than one million of South Sudan's six million have fled their homes and the country is on the brink of famine. The UN supported by the EU has set up five refugee camps. So international organisations have been effective in feeding and protecting refugees but it has not been effective in preventing the civil war. However the blame lies with the new ruling elite of South Sudan.

To conclude, international organisations such as the UN and the EU have made some major progress in promoting development in African countries on a small scale, but they have faced problems overall development because of the vast problems the continent faces like hunger and lack of education. The situation in South Sudan highlights the difficulties facing international organisation, despite massive international aid the country is in ruin.

Marker's comment

This is an excellent answer as it covers a range of points. The structure of the answer clarifies the issue with clear and consistent lines of argument. A range of developed points with accurate analytical comments are made that are justified and exemplified. It provides excellent up-to-date exemplification. This answer also provides balance by offering counter-arguments that are relevant and insightful. The conclusion is balanced and insightful and directly addresses the central part of the question. Full marks.

Analyse

Section 3, Option 1: World Power

Question

Analyse the effective of policies designed to tackle inequality in the World Power you have studied. **12 marks**

Responses will be credited that make reference to:

- policies introduced to tackle the issue
- success/effectiveness or otherwise of these policies
- analysis/evaluation of the policies.

Model answer

Social inequalities still exist in the USA with some groups more likely to suffer social and economic inequality than others. Black people and Hispanics are more likely to be poorer, be unemployed, die younger and to under achieve in education. They are also more likely to be in trouble with the police and to spend time in prison. Various US governments and presidents have tried to tackle some of these inequalities at both a federal and state level. Some of the attempts at reducing inequality include initiatives and policies such as No Child Left Behind, Obamacare, Temporary Assistance for Needy Families and the American Recovery and Reinvestment Act. Some of these policies have had more than success than others.

One policy that can be viewed as having some success is the Patient Protection and Affordable Care Act (Obamacare). This was introduced in 2010 to increase the quality and affordability of health insurance, to lower the number of Americans without healthcare coverage and to reduce health inequalities. Obamacare has meant that 7 million more Americans have healthcare cover but it has a long way to go as around 40 million Americans still don't have any cover. Critics of Obamacare call it socialised medicine and see it as evidence of the Government interfering in Americans' lives. However, the policy has proven to be very popular with America's poor and impoverished ethnic minorities and could have a positive impact on the morbidity and mortality rates of the poorest Americans.

With the election of President Trump, the future of Obamacare is in doubt as he has pledged to either reform or replace the policy.

Another policy is Temporary Assistance for Needy Families (TANF). This is a federal programme implemented by individual states. It is aimed at getting more single parents back into employment with welfare payments being linked to the efforts of those seeking work. TANF is only available for 5 years but since it has been introduced, the poverty rate among single parents has fallen. This shows TANF's effectiveness, but recently the number of people receiving TANF has fallen as the entry requirements have increased. Despite TANF's success, the USA still has one of the highest rates of child poverty in the developed world. This shows the programme has had some success but still has a long way to go before it can claim to be fully successful.

A final policy is the American Recovery and Reinvestment Act which was introduced to counter the global economic crash of 2008. The Act was based largely on proposals put forward by President Obama and was intended to improve the US economy and maintain employment and income standards by pumping $787 billion into the US economy in the form of tax cuts, expansion of unemployment benefits and an increase on domestic spending such as schools, roads, hospitals, etc. Many of those who benefitted were poor black people and Hispanics who saw an increase in employment rates as ⇨

well as income. That said, unemployment rates are still higher than they were before the recession and it will take a while before they are back to the pre-recession levels. This shows that the Act has not yet had the intended impact as it has taken too long and that many Americans, particularly black people and Hispanics, are still struggling with a variety of social and economic inequalities.

Marker's comments

A good awareness of the types of policies and initiatives to tackle social inequalities. A good awareness of their impact on individual groups. Good awareness too of the impact Donald Trump's presidency may have on these policies. Full marks.

Evaluate

Section 2, Option 1: Social Inequality

Question

Answer may refer to Scotland **or** the United Kingdom or both.

Evaluate the main factors that influence health inequalities. **12 marks**

Responses will be credited that make reference to:

- individualist and collectivist views on health inequalities
- the influence of poverty and social inequality on health inequalities
- the influence of lifestyle choices on health inequalities.

Up to 8 marks for knowledge (description, explanation and exemplification) and up to 4 marks for evaluation and structured answers.

Model answer

It is self-evident that poor lifestyle choices such as smoking, drinking to excess and poor diet impact on an individual's health. This is the view of those who support the individualist approach which states that an individual's lifestyle choices are responsible for their health. In contrast, the collectivist viewpoint is that poverty and social inequality are the driving forces which lead to poor lifestyle choices.

Parts of Scotland are blighted by a 'booze culture' which according to the NHS kills 40 Scots a week. The 2017 Scottish Health Survey indicated that Scots are more likely than drinkers elsewhere in Britain both to binge on alcohol and exceed the recommended daily intake. Daily alcohol consumption in Scotland for both men and women is 25 per cent higher than in England. This is despite health promotion campaigns to persuade the public to drink in moderation. The SNP Government has

passed legislation to introduce alcohol minimum unit pricing and this finally was introduced in 2018.

Obesity and smoking are also a lifestyle choice and as a result more and more Scots are becoming obese. It is estimated that over 3000 Scots die every year as a direct result of obesity and there are more than 13,000 smoking-related deaths. (There is a clear link between smoking and lung cancer.)

However, it is clear that obesity and smoking and alcohol abuse are social class and poverty issues. While the number of women in Social Class I who are obese is about 13%, the figure for Social Class V is over 25%. Obesity is linked to heart disease, diabetes and premature death. The figures for smoking also display the wealth/poverty divide. According to the 2017 Scottish Households Survey, 35% of people living in the most deprived areas smoke cigarettes, compared to only 10% in the least deprived area. ⇨

The SNP Government's Equally Well report on health inequalities concludes 'that there is a clear relationship between income inequality and health inequality'. It states that more than two-thirds of the total alcohol-related deaths were in the most deprived areas and that those living in the most deprived areas of Scotland have a suicide risk double that of the Scottish average. It is difficult to make lifestyle choices when you are unemployed, living in poor housing and in a deprived area. Membership of a gym, private healthcare, health foods and a jog in the park belong to a different world.

Overall and most importantly, it is clear that poor lifestyle choices occur as a direct result of poverty, making poverty the most important factor contributing to poor health. Furthermore, poverty does not only lead to poor lifestyle choices but impacts badly on the mental health of those who experience social deprivation.

Marker's comments

This is an excellent answer because it is rich in knowledge and evaluation. The introduction links the individualist/collectivist debate to the main explanation of lifestyle choices and poverty. Each point is fully developed with relevant up-to-date description and explanation. The impact of obesity, smoking and especially of alcohol are fully developed and, impressively, are also linked to poverty and social inequality. Full marks.

Chapter 14
Unlocking the source-based marks

In this question paper, you will need to answer three source-based questions. These are:

- To what extent is it accurate to state that … (objectivity question)
- What conclusions can be drawn … (conclusions question)
- To what extent are sources … (reliability question).

There are 28 marks available and candidates have 1 hour 15 minutes to complete this paper.

The marks breakdown for each question is as follows:

Objectivity questions (10 marks)

- Up to 3 marks for a single developed point, depending on the use of the evidence in the sources and the quality of the analysis or evaluation.
- For full marks you must refer to all sources in your answer.
- You must also make an overall judgement as to the extent of the accuracy of the given statement.
- You can only achieve a maximum of 8 marks if no overall judgement is made on extent of accuracy of the statement.

Conclusions questions (10 marks)

- Up to 3 marks for a single developed point depending on the use of the evidence in the sources and the quality of the analysis or evaluation.
- For full marks you must refer to all sources in your answer.
- You are required to make an overall conclusion about the issue in the question.
- You can only achieve a maximum of 8 marks if you do not provide an overall conclusion.

Reliability questions (8 marks)

- Up to 2 marks for a single developed point, depending on the use of the evidence in the sources and the quality of the analysis and/or evaluation.
- For full marks you must refer to all sources in your answer.
- You must also make a judgement based on the evidence in the most reliable source. A maximum of 6 marks can be awarded if you do not provide an overall judgement.
- A maximum of 3 marks can be awarded if only one factor is considered, for example, date, bias, sample size, provenance.

The fully worked out examples for each of the three source skills questions on the following pages show you how to tackle the source questions and to maximise the marks available.

Exam tip

Time management is extremely important. Candidates should spend no more than:

✓ 21 minutes on the 8-mark question
✓ 27 minutes on each of the 10-mark questions.

Questions and model answers
Objectivity question (10 marks)

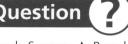

Question

Study Sources A, B and C then attempt the question that follows.

Source A

Zero-hour contracts allow employers to hire staff with no set working hours. This means employees work only when they are needed by their employer, often at short notice. Payment depends on hours worked. This benefits employers as it reduces their wage bill and can increase profits. However, it can lead to a high turnover of staff and can impact on productivity. This type of work contract is being increasingly used by employers. In 2016 the figure stood at an estimated 900,000 compared to 650,000 in 2013. This represents 3% of the UK workforce. Well-known companies such as McDonald's and Sports Direct use these contracts as do the NHS and charities. Zero-hour contracts are higher among young people than other age groups, with 37% of those employed on such contracts aged between 16 and 24.

The CBI (Confederation of Business Industry) argues that zero-hour contracts have played an important part in Britain's economic recovery and its having one of the lowest unemployment rates in Europe – in Spain, for example, 50% of those under 25 are unemployed. The CBI states 'flexible contracts provide opportunities for work to help people build careers. They offer a choice to those who want flexibility in the hours they work, such as students, retired people, parents and carers'. The major users of these contracts are in accommodations and food and in administrative and support services. Employers argue that zero-hour contracts provide affordable services to the public as well as employment. Many services in the tourist industry, for example, need this flexibility to survive and provide crucial employment in rural areas. The CBI also states that many employees enjoy working with these contracts.

The Trade Union Congress (TUC) argues that many workers on zero-hour contracts are at risk of exploitation and 'for many workers they mean poverty pay and no way of knowing how often they'll be working from week to week'. Again, many workers on zero-hour contracts are prevented from taking other employment even if they are only working for four hours a week, as their signed contracts state that employees must be available for work. These contracts mean employers avoid redundancy pay and pension contributions, with workers often unable to obtain credit references, loans or mortgages. Workers on these contracts would prefer guaranteed weekly hours and a significant number would prefer more hours. Many workers who achieve limited hours of work are forced to use food banks and to take out loans with very high interest rates.

Source: adapted from www.bbc.co.uk

Source B

Survey findings of employment satisfaction for zero-hour and non-zero-hour workers

Issue	Zero-hour contract %	Non-zero-hour contract %
Satisfied with job	60	59
Work–life balance	65	58
Treated unfairly	27	29
Prefer more hours	40	10

Source: adapted from Chartered Institute of Personnel and Development (CIPD) and other sources (2015)

Source C

Gross weekly pay and average hours per week for zero-hour and non-zero-hour workers

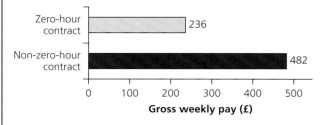

Gross weekly pay (£)

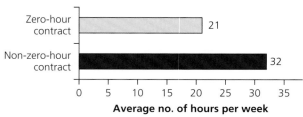

Average no. of hours per week

Source: Resolution Foundation (an independent research and policy organisation) and other sources (2015)

Attempt the following question, using only the information in Sources A, B and C.
To what extent is it accurate to state that zero-hour contracts benefit only the employer? **8 marks**

In your answer, you may wish to evaluate the reliability of the sources.

Model answer

Evidence to support the view that zero-hour contracts benefit only the employers can be found in Sources A, B and C.

Source A states that these contracts benefit the employer as the employer has lower wage bills and can make higher profits. This is backed up with further evidence from Source A which states that the TUC believes that the contracts can lead to poverty pay. This is further backed up with evidence also from Source C which shows that those not on zero-hour contracts receive a much higher level of pay, with an average of £482 per week compared to £236 for those with zero-hour contracts. This evidence shows that employers do benefit greatly from this type of contract.

Further evidence for this view can be found in Sources B and C. Source B shows that a large minority of those on these types of contracts (40%) would prefer to work longer hours and this is backed up with evidence from Source C that shows that those on zero-hour contracts work fewer hours than those on other types of contracts. This evidence shows that zero-hour contracts benefit employers more than employees.

However, there is also evidence that zero-hour contracts benefit employees rather than employers.

Source A states that the CBI believes that zero-hour contracts have helped aid economic recovery and have led to the creation of many jobs which means that more people are in employment, particularly young workers. This is backed up with evidence from Source A which shows that over one-third of young workers (37%) are now employed in jobs which have zero-hour contracts and this allows many young workers greater flexibility which means they can work but also continue in university or college education. This is further backed up by evidence from Source B which shows that this has created a greater work–life balance for many workers. This evidence shows that it is not just employers that benefit from zero-hour contracts.

Further evidence for this view can be found in the sources. There is a high level of workers satisfied with zero-hour contracts which links back to Source A that many employees enjoy working these types of contracts. Also, zero-hour contracts can have a negative impact on employers as they

tend to have a high turnover of staff which could be costly to them.

Overall, the statement is mostly correct as these contracts provide far more benefits to the employer than to the employee, such as increased profits and lower costs, as employees with zero-hour contracts are paid significantly less than those with other contracts. This clearly benefits employers more than it does the employee.

Marker's comments

An excellent response. Great use of sources with information used between and within the sources and evidence from the sources used to back up any point made. Also, a very thorough and detailed overall evaluation which makes a clear decision on the extent of how much the statement is supported by the sources. Full marks.

Conclusions question (10 marks)

Question ?

Study Sources A, B and C, then attempt the question that follows.

Source A

Female representation in Scottish and UK politics

Across Europe there has been varying degrees of success in terms of female representation in Parliament. In July 2016, Theresa May became the new leader of the Conservative Party and thus the new prime minister of the UK. This followed on from Nicola Sturgeon becoming the first minister of Scotland in 2014.

At the 2015 UK general election a record number of female Members of Parliament (MPs) were elected to the UK Parliament from 650 MPs. This highlights the progress that is being made (in the 2010 general election 144 female MPs were elected). Today over one in four MPs are female compared to less than one in ten in 1992.

Outside the House of Commons, just over a quarter of the members of the House of Lords are women. In the National Assembly for Wales 42% of the representatives are female, although this is down from around half of the Assembly Members (AMs) 15 years ago when the Welsh Assembly was established. In the European Parliament 41% of the UK Members of the European Parliament (MEPs) are women. In local government in Scotland the number of female councillors has remained static at around 24% for a number of years. In contrast 32% of local councillors in England are women.

In the Scottish Parliament women make up around a third of the Members of the Scottish Parliament (MSPs). After the 2016 Scottish Parliament election, the figure remained the same. Disappointingly, this number is lower than when the Scottish Parliament was established in 1999.

Across the UK the main political parties have different levels of female representation. The Labour Party in Scotland and the UK has, for many years, had a policy of trying to return more female MPs through the use of all-female candidate shortlists. This explains why Labour has the highest percentage of female MPs and MSPs. The Conservative Party and the Liberal Democrat Party claim they would like to see more women representatives elected in their respective parties. However, many Conservative Party local associations oppose women-only shortlists, preferring to persuade more women to stand as candidates. The Liberal Democrats are opposed to women-only shortlists.

In both the UK and Scottish Cabinets there has been an increase in the number of female ministers. Currently there are eight women in the UK Cabinet (including the prime minister). The highest number under David Cameron was seven. After the 2016 Holyrood election, Nicola Sturgeon appointed a gender balance Cabinet of five women and five men (in the previous Cabinet around 40% of ministers were female). This new Cabinet has the highest female Scottish Cabinet representation since the Scottish Parliament was set up. At the SNP party conference in 2014, Ms Sturgeon stated she wanted to see something closer to half the ministers in the Scottish Cabinet as female with half the MSPs also women. In the 2016 Scottish elections, the percentage of SNP female MSPs who were elected was the highest ever.

Source B

Male and female representation in Parliaments

UK

Election year	Female MPs	%	Male MPs	%
1997	120	18.2	539	81.8
2001	118	17.9	541	82.1
2005	127	19.5	522	80.5
2010	144	22.2	505	77.8
2015	191	29.4	458	70.6

Scotland

Election year	Female MPs	%	Male MPs	%
1999	48	36.0	81	64.0
2003	51	39.5	78	60.5
2007	43	33.4	86	66.6
2011	45	34.9	84	65.1
2016	45	34.9	84	65.1

Selected European countries

Country	Percentage female	Percentage male
Germany	31	69
France	39	61
Ireland	22	78
Norway	41.4	58.6
Denmark	37.4	62.6
Spain	39.1	60.9
Italy	34	66
Czechia	22	78

Source C

	Number of female MSPs/MPs by party				Percentage of party total			
	Lab	Con	Lib Dem	SNP	Lab	Con	Lib Dem	SNP
MSPs (Scotland)	11	6	0	27	45	19	0	43
MPs (UK)	99	68	0	23	43	20	0	41

Attempt the following question, using only the information in Sources A, B and C.

What conclusions can be drawn about the representation of women in Scottish and UK politics?

You must draw one conclusion about each of the following:

- the representation of women in the Scottish Parliament compared to the UK Parliament
- the representation of women in the main political parties in Scotland and the UK
- the representation of women in Scottish and UK Parliaments in comparison with selected European Parliaments.

You must give an overall conclusion about the representation of women in Scottish and UK politics. **8 marks**

Model answer

A conclusion that can be made about the representation of women in the Scottish Parliament compared to the UK is that Scotland still has a higher number of female representatives than those in the UK despite the gap narrowing significantly. The evidence for this can be found in Sources A and B. Source A states that in 2015 almost 30% of MPs were female which is a trebling of the figure from 1992 whereas the number of female MSPs has not increased since 2003 and is fewer than the original number when the Scottish Parliament was created (Source B). This is backed up by evidence in Source B which shows the percentage of female representation in the UK Parliament has risen from 18.2% in 1997 to 29% in 2015 and in Scotland the figure has fallen from 36.0% in 1999 to 34.9% in 2016. Despite this fall, Scotland still has a higher percentage of female elected representatives.

A conclusion that can be made about the representation of women in the main political parties is that there are varying levels of female representation across the parties. The evidence

for this can be found in Sources A and C. Source A states that the Labour Party tries to promote women in politics by having all-women shortlists whereas parties such as the Conservatives and the Lib Dems tend not to favour all-women shortlists. Also in Source A, it states that the SNP has a policy of wanting more female representatives in government and wants to see half the ministers being female. Source C backs this up by showing statistics for each party which highlights the differences between the parties and the different approaches. These different approaches could help explain the reason why the parties have differing levels of female representation.

A conclusion that can be made about the representation of UK and Scottish MPs and MSPs compared to European countries is that some countries are doing much better than the UK and Scotland but that Scotland seems more in line with most of the European countries compared to the UK. Some European countries though are doing much better than others. The evidence for this can be found in Sources A and B. Source A

157

states that, 'Across Europe there has been varying degrees of success in terms of female representation in Parliament.' This is backed up with evidence from Source B which shows that countries such as France, Spain and Norway have figures around 40% whereas Ireland and Czechia have just above one in 5 representatives who are female. Scotland has around 34% and the UK is around 30%.

An overall conclusion is that women remain under-represented in both Scottish and UK politics, having less than half the representatives at any level, except the Scottish Government

Cabinet which has an equal number of men to women. Between Scotland and the UK, the gap is narrowing as the number of MPs that are female increases and the number of female MSPs decreases.

Marker's comment

A very good response for each of the conclusions. Good use of source evidence from between and within sources and very good synthesis and justification provided for each of the conclusions. The overall conclusion is also very thorough and detailed. Full marks.

Reliability question (8 marks)

Question ?

Study Sources A, B and C, then attempt the question that follows.

Source A

Interview with British jihadi in Syria:

What made you leave the UK? What was the deciding factor?

To come to Syria. To leave *dar al kufr* [the land of disbelievers].

Why are you out in Syria?

To spread the religion of Allah and to help Muslims. I can speak Arabic and English. That's like my only skill. I've spent efforts to take down the Syrian government. That's all I want to say.

Have you joined Isis?

I'm not Isis, but I believe in the Sharia. I believe we should follow Islam how the first Muslims did. I also think that whatever I say, the media will probably freestyle with it and make up more nicknames for me as a result of the void they have in their lives.

What do you think about Isis? Can you give us an insight into what's going on in Syria with Isis? They've recently released a video saying they'll attack the UK — what are your thoughts on that?

I'm doing my own thing. I don't focus that much on what Isis does. Also this may sound strange but this is genuinely the first time someone's told me they threatened to attack the UK, which is probably a bit embarrassing, seeing as I'm in Syria and you'd expect I'd hear these things. If Britain stopped bombing Muslims in Syria the Muslims in Syria would stop attacking them. Is that hard to understand?

Source: *The Independent, 'Jihadi Jack' Letts interview: Former Oxford schoolboy calls on British people to convert to Islam as he brands David Cameron an 'evil creature' by Shebab Khan, published 30 January 2016.*

⇨ Source B

Public opinion survey: issues facing Britain

What do you see as the biggest issue facing the UK today?

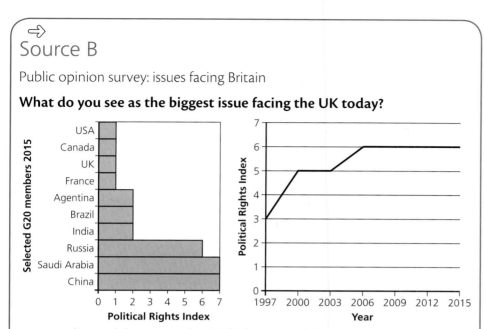

(7 = People have very weak political rights, 1 = People have very strong political rights)

Source: Ipsos MORI interviewed a representative quota sample of 1011 adults aged 18+ across Great Britain, 7–20 January 2016.

Source C

Channel 4 website

Source: Channel 4 News website, 'Do we know why we are in Afghanistan?' by Jon Snow, published 28 July 2009.

Attempt the following question, using only the information in Sources A, B and C.

To what extent are Sources A, B and C reliable?

You must provide an overall conclusion on the most reliable source of information.

Model answer

Source A

Source A can be seen as not being reliable as it is a one sided and potentially biased view from someone who is campaigning or fighting on behalf of someone. This means that the view is one sided and there is no opposing view to the one stated. That said, the article is fairly up to date so it might contain some information which is relevant.

Source B

Source B can be seen to be reliable because it came from Ipsos Mori which is a professional and highly reputable polling organisation that is well known for using proper research methods. This can be seen in the large sample size used by them to sample the public's opinion. The information was also gained by asking a representative sample which means that it could be seen as being reliable as it reflects the views of adults across the UK.

Source C

Source C can be seen to be not very reliable as it comes from 2009 and the information in the source could be out of date and have changed since 2009. That said, Channel 4 News and Jon Snow are two very reputable journalistic sources. Channel 4 can be seen to be a professional news organisation and Jon Snow is a much-respected journalist.

Overall

Source B can be seen to be the most reliable as it comes from a reputable polling organisation that has used a wide sample and large number of people in order to give a true reflection of what the public think. It is also up to date unlike Source C. Source A is too one sided and biased in order to be fully reliable.

Marker's comment

Each source is very detailed and contains good evidence in support of or against their reliability. The overall evaluation discusses all three sources and compares them in order to make a judgement about which one is the most reliable. Full marks.

Acknowledgements

The publishers are grateful for the use of material on **pp.143–144** taken from the SQA Higher Modern Studies Course Specification. Copyright © Scottish Qualifications Authority. Exam question copyright **pp.158–159** © Scottish Qualifications Authority. *Please note that the model answer does not emanate from SQA.*

p.38 Quotation from DWP spokesperson reproduced with kind permission of the Press Association; **p.39** Quotation from Jamie Livingstone, head of Oxfam Scotland, taken from [https://oxfamapps.org/scotland/2014/06/09/2014-06-big-rise-in-uk-food-poverty-seesmore-than-20m-meals-given-out-in-last-year/] is reproduced with the permission of Oxfam, Oxfam House, John Smith Drive, Cowley, Oxford OX4 2JY, UK www.oxfam.org.uk. *Oxfam does not necessarily endorse any text or activities that accompany the materials;* **p.47** An extract from p14 of 'Equally Well: Report of the Ministerial Task Force on Health Inequalities' produced by The Scottish Government 2008 (http://www.scotland.gov.uk/Resource/Doc/229649/0062206.pdf) © Crown copyright 2008. Contains public sector information licensed under the Open Government Licence v3.0; **p.62** Extracts taken from http://www.scra.gov.uk/publications/online_statistical_service.cfm © Scottish Children's Reporter Administration and http://www.scra.gov.uk/children_s_hearings_system/index.cfm © Children's Hearings Scotland; **p.67** An extract adapted from the article 'More than 5000 join anti-rape midnight protest' by Martin Williams, from The Herald, 10 June 2014 © Herald & Times Group; **pp.69–70** Extracts from www.gov.uk and www.sps.gov.uk © Crown Copyright. Contains public sector information licensed under the Open Government Licence v3.0; **p.81** Data taken from www.kff.org/other/state-indicator/poverty-rate-byraceethnicity © Henry J Kaiser Foundation, and the US Census Bureau. *Please note that this product uses the Census Bureau Data API but is not endorsed or certified by the Census Bureau;* **p.105** An extract from The Fall of the ANC by Prince Mashele and Mzukisi Qobo, published by Picador Africa 2014, an imprint of Pan Macmillan; **pp.158–9** Source A: Article is adapted from '"Jihadi Jack" Letts interview: Former Oxford schoolboy calls on British people to convert to Islam as he brands David Cameron an "evil creature"' by Shebab Khan, taken from The Independent, 30 January 2016; Source B: Graph is adapted from 'Issues facing Britain – What do you see as the biggest issue facing the UK today?' © Ipsos MORI; Source C: Screenshot of Channel 4 News website – "Do we know why we're in Afghanistan" by Jon Snow, 28 July 2009 © Channel 4 TV.

Data sources are acknowledged, where relevant, throughout the text. Unless otherwise specified, data used in the creation of graphics throughout this book is public domain.